THE OFFICIAL TENNESSEE BOOK

C000094087

They Said It
Their Way

Edwin Garrett

PUBLISHED B Y FIDELI PUBLISHING INC.

ISBN: 978-1-60414-953-1

———

For information, please contact
Fideli Publishing, Inc.:
info@fidelipublishing.com
www.FideliPublishing.com

An Introduction and Guide to Understanding This Collection

I have always loved the written word and reading but, never **in all my born days** did I ever expect to write a book. The idea to do so emerged so slowly that I was taking notes and writing down old sayings and by-words long before the notion occurred to organize them into something that would be meaningful and interesting enough that others would want to read it.

There were three strong influences that caused this to happen. Soon after our people were introduced to television in the 1950s, I began to notice a change in the way the younger children were speaking. They didn't sound like they were **from around here.**

The Southern accents we were accustomed to hearing were rapidly disappearing and a new and different vernacular was emerging. I became more aware of this change when my first two grandsons were growing up next door to my wife, Peg, and me. They certainly spoke, and still do, with an accent that was radically different from that which I heard when I was a boy growing up in the Cedar Grove community of rural Middle Tennessee.

The second influence was learning a few computer skills and the purchase of a computer. This magnificent invention alleviated much of the time consuming labor of manual handwriting and laborious research, and opened a door that made the process easier and more time efficient. I doubt that I would ever have attempted such a task without this help.

The third and greatest influence was the desire to pass down to my posterity some of the customs and ways that I enjoyed so much when I was a young boy. I want my three grandsons, my granddaughter, and my three great grandsons and my great-granddaughter to know about their ancestry and the way we lived in the wonderfully simple time that I now refer to as **the barefooted days**.

So as you begin to read this quaint collection of by-words, old sayings, phrases, and stories, which are unique for the most part to a particular section of Tennessee, readers may wonder about the sounds, meaning, and spelling of the words.

Please note that most of the stories and by-words are from a bygone day, a time when children attended one-teacher schools, when there were very few automobiles; an era when it was a rarity to see an airplane fly across the sky, and upon being heard, children would race out of the schoolhouse to get a glimpse of it.

Many of the population of the Cedar Grove community, home of the author, were share croppers while a few were subsistence farmers who raised all their food and employed some of the husband and wife share croppers.

There were no monthly utility bills to pay. Electricity was not yet available to rural areas and households had either a well or carried their water from cool, mountain springs. Those who owned land fared well and often reached out to help their neighbors.

Readers are alerted to this oddity: There are words in this collection of sayings, such as *splouzed* (rhyme with blouse), *scrouged* (rhyme with gouged), and **scrootch** (rhyme with pooch) which were attempts by the author to capture correct phonetic sounds and it's probable that many of these words had never been written down. Some of the words go back to Bible days and their meanings can easily be construed from the context while the origin of others is just a guess. As you read these pages, be reminded that most of the time "they" and "their" refer to those in the title, *They Said It Their Way*.

All the stories and poems included in this collection are true with the exception of those in some of the **Phrase in use** and **Commentaries** sections. A few names were changed to avoid any embarrassment to friends or relatives. So, in alphabetical order (well, nearly) let's remember how...

Edwin Garrett

They Said It Their Way

A

A bad egg

Meaning: An unsavory person, one of bad character. Often was heard spoken in the author's household in the olden days.

Phrase in use: A country singer/songwriter, Johnny Russell, wrote a line in one of his songs that describes **a bad egg** very well. He wrote: "Don't be hanging around old Catfish John." It could be assumed that Catfish John was **a bad egg,** although in the song, it turned out he was a pretty good guy.

A cat on wheels

Meaning: A spirited or vivacious personality.

Phrase in use: Recently said of Dana Halsell, my wife's cousin, who posted her picture on Facebook. Dana was dressed in Halloween garb and it was remarked, she's **a cat on wheels** making reference to her vivacious personality. Other connotations of the phrase could be in connection with a mean or unruly child or young lady who was considered to be a little "fast."

A Chinaman's chance

Meaning: His chances are very slim.

Phrase in use: Commonly heard in how good a person's chances or opportunities were. **A Chinaman's chance** meant his chances were nil.

A 'coon's age

Meaning: A very long period of time.

Phrase in use: Often stated upon seeing an old friend who hadn't been seen in years. "You haven't been around in **a 'coon's age**." Now it is not known exactly how long a 'coon lives, but if this phrase makes reference to that animal, it could be assumed they live to a ripe old age.

A duke's mixture

Meaning: Containing many ingredients.

Phrase in use: If the baby has his mother's eyes, his daddy's big ears, and his uncle's red hair, he's probably **a duke's mixture** of several bloodlines.

A forn thing

Meaning: Not one single, solitary thing.

Phrase in use: When his neighbors had a dispute over their land, Fate certainly didn't want to be involved and he told them that he didn't know **a forn thing** about their property line. But they kept trying to drag him into their squabble until they did, then both sides got fighting mad at good ole Fate.

A ghost of a chance

Meaning: The possibility is almost nil, and like the Chinaman's chance, slim to none.

Phrase in use: He hasn't **a ghost of a chance** to win that fight, but like this writer's cousin, little Billy, he'll fight 'til the end and never give up.

Commentary: Prize fighting was a popular sport with our people especially when there were very few radios in the community

3

during the late 1930s and throughout WWII days. Neighbors would congregate at Chat and Margie Garrett's store on Friday nights just to hear the War news or listen to Joe Louis beat up some new challenger.

There was still much prejudice at that time, and some would be against the mighty Louis merely because of his color. Many, however, idolized him and would adamantly state that any challenger didn't stand **a ghost of a chance** against the Brown Bomber.

How strange it seems now that despite the hero worship he had earned, most of his followers would not have allowed the famous fighter to drink from the common dipper in the bucket of drinking water that hung on their front porches.

A good old do-nothing feller

Meaning: The fellow was just OK. This saying was unique to my father-in-law, Dewey Robbins.

Phrase in use: Dewey once said this about the sheriff of Overton County: Stated Dewey, "Yeah, I guess I'll vote for him again, he's been **a good old do-nothing sheriff.**"

A good talking to

Meaning: A scolding.

Phrase in use: Someone needs to give Elvie's kids **a good talking to** or they'll be completely out of hand before school starts next fall.

A high class way of begging

Meaning: A way to gain favors without really asking. This was my daddy's opinion of bridal and baby showers and unique to him. He hated those showers and was not shy in stating his opinion of them.

Phrase in use: Daddy thought that giving a shower was just **a high class way of begging**. The older I get the more amazed I become by the psyche of a woman. My wife, Peggy, still has a few of the items we received at our wedding shower, and after 62 years she can still remember who gave them.

A little bird told me

Meaning: I learned your secret but I won't tell you how I found out.

Phrase in use: When some lovesick boy asked, "How did you know I have a crush on Joanie?" there came this reply, "**A little bird told me.**"

Commentary: As a boy I remember the many species of birds that inhabited the woods and the fields and a cacophony of their beautiful songs rang through the hills. When a Redbird (Cardinal) was spotted this little verse was usually recited, specifically by those who might have a girlfriend: *Redbird, Redbird fly to the right, see my sweetheart, 'fore tonight.*

A month of Sundays

Meaning: A very long time.

Phrase in use: All I know is that he's been gone for what seems like **a month of Sundays.**

Commentary: Since a month is 30 or 31 days, I suppose **a month of Sundays** would be 30 or 31 Sundays adding up to that many weeks.

A pack of lies

Meaning: Just one falsehood after another with no truth to it.

Phrase in use: The incumbent told **a pack of lies** to try and get re-elected, but it backfired on him and his opponent won the election.

Commentary: Henry Ford once said, "History is **a pack of lies** agreed on."

A time and again

Meaning: Taking a very long time to complete.

Phrase in use: Aunt Sade thought it was taking her children a very long time. She said, "**It's taking a time and again** for them kids to get home from school today and they'll smell the patching when they do get here."

A trick with a hole in it

Meaning: A person who is shifty and untrustworthy.

Phrase in use: Many times Dewey was known to say, "Don't believe a word he says, he's **a trick with a hole in it.**"

A Wampus cat

Meaning: (Sometimes spoken: "*Wampus cat with a bob-wire tail*"). A tough or unruly person who braggingly referred to himself as this just prior to a fight or right after it had happened. Sometimes used as a warning or to try and bluff the opponent out of the fight.

Phrase in use: "Watch out for him, because he's **a Wampus cat!**" Reply, "No, he's a **Wampus cat with a bob wire tail***!*"

Commentary: Barbed wire was called "bob" wire in earlier times and is thus called by some still.

7

A waterhaul

Meaning: To fail or come back empty handed.

Phrase in use: We drove 80 miles trying to buy corn for our livestock and made **a waterhaul**.

Commentary: Once when I was a very young boy Daddy and I drove to Celina and on up the Obey River to Willow Grove looking for corn to buy for our livestock. It had been extremely dry that summer and most everyone's corn crops had failed; therefore, we made **a waterhaul**. If we tried to retrace that route today, we'd have to travel by boat. All of that land is now covered with water because of the Dale Hollow Dam which was built during WWII.

About to give down

Meaning: Sick, weak, or frail and just about done for.

Phrase in use: John says poor old Aunt Surrie is just **about to give down**. He says she's been acting poorly all winter long and may not last until spring if this cold weather lingers too long.

Across the waters

Meaning: Across the ocean or the sea.

Phrase in use: Johnny won't be back for a long time. He's **across the waters** now fighting the Germans.

A'fixin' to

Meaning: Preparing, getting ready, or intending to act.

Phrase in use: Jaime was always **a'fixin to** get ready but was never ready on time.

A'fore

Meaning: The same as "before."

Phrase in use: We country boys were always a little skittish of the town boys and never wanted to get into any trouble because we were scared of the law. We managed to always get out of there **a'fore** any trouble started, sometimes leaving earlier than had been intended. However, things did change when we started high school and became friends with them.

9

Again'

Meaning: Against. It meant the same as the original word except, they left off the "st."

Phrase in use: I told my cousins we'd better get a move on or supper's going to be over **again'** the time we get home and I didn't want to miss supper. Came the reply, "Let's step it up a bit. I'm hungry too, and Granny Garrett sets a mighty fine table, especially when you're doing her a favor like we are."

Commentary: That was their language trademark, make it shorter. No use wasting energy on extra syllables or words.

Ailing

Meaning: Many old timers used this word in lieu of "ill" when referring to a person as being "poorly" or "under the weather."

Phrase in use: In speaking it might have been used in this manner: "Uncle Zeke's not feeling well a 'tall." And the likely reply, "Yeah, he's been **ailing** most of the winter."

Commentary: This word brings to mind a story my parents used to tell about my cousin James Buck. When James was just a boy, Uncle J.T. was teaching him to chop out corn.

It was a hot July day and Cousin James was feeling great when they went into the field. He felt like a man carrying that gooseneck hoe over his shoulder like his daddy. However, James began to feel sick before they had finished the first long row. He said he was **ailing** and was soon down on his all-fours trying to throw up. He was released from his duties for the day and told to go on home and rest until he was feeling better.

Later, when his daddy came home for dinner, that's the noon meal in those parts, James was not to be seen. Inquiring about how the boy was feeling, Aunt Dona was surprised and said that he never mentioned being sick to her. It seems James had made a miraculous recovery. Aunt Dona said he came in, ate up all the beans she had cooked for supper, then went outside to play and hadn't been seen since.

After a brief search was made about the premises they decided to look around the barn. They were just about to give up the search and call in the neighbors when Aunt Dona thought she heard a noise that sounded somewhat like snoring or maybe the big hog that was being fattened for slaughter, grunting. Upon closer examination they noticed the hog rooting around his feed trough very much awake.

Soon little James was found in the hay loft fast asleep and snoring loudly. But be assured, he didn't sleep very long. He was soon getting a dose of hickory tea.

Ain't got sense enough to stay out of the fire

Meaning: Not very smart.

Phrase in use: Sometimes you children act as though you **ain't got sense enough to stay out of the fire.**

Ain't much punkin'

Meaning: Feeling poorly.

Phrase in use: "I **ain't much punkin'** today," groaned Pa Bell.

Ain't no skin off my nose

Meaning: Lack of empathy.

Phrase in use: If Luke gets burnt in his trade with Fowler, it **ain't no skin off my nose,** because he was duly warned about dealing with an old mule trader.

Commentary: When the writer was Principal at Allons Elementary School, he and his close friend, the late H.C. Langford taught there together. There was a boy in his room who was a real bully. Big Barry loved to pick on the younger and smaller children, especially Little George.

H.C. would often say, "One day, Little George will grow a bit and give Big Barry the whipping he deserves, and when that happens I'll just turn my head and not see a thing."

Well, sure enough, one autumn day not long after the new school year began, the younger boy had hit a growth spurt during the summer and when Big Barry started a fight he learned the hard way that bullying does not pay. This time he was on the losing end, with a bloody nose and a black eye.

True to his word, although standing nearby, the crafty old teacher didn't see a thing until all the children gave a large round of applause. Don't you just know H.C. was thinking, "It **ain't no skin off my nose."**

The writer also states that H.C. was an excellent teacher and possessed great musical ability. He always had a student choir in which every member was auditioned before he could join. Sadly for some, they did not make the cut.

Ain't seen hide nor hair of him

Meaning: The person or thing hasn't been seen nor heard from for a long while, or in other words, completely out of sight.

Phrase in use: Old George is missing and we **ain't seen hide nor hair of him** in over a week.

Commentary: This brings to mind a true story that was passed down from my grandfather, Martin Garrett. Joe Nation was at Martin Garrett's farm often and worked there along with several other hired hands. One day it was noted that Joe Nation was missing and no one had **seen hide nor hair of him** for several weeks.

Soon word spread throughout the community that he was dead, but a few weeks later, much to the surprise of everyone, Joe showed up at the Garrett place very much alive.

"Why Joe Nation!" Pa Garrett exclaimed! "We heard you were dead!"

"I heard that too," replied Joe Nation, "but I knew it wasn't so as soon as I heard it."

Air

Meaning: One hour.

Phrase in use: Tell your ma not to wait supper for us because it'll take about an **air** for us to finish this job. But be sure to tell her to save plenty of the leftovers because this is a hungry bunch of boys she'll be feeding. She can put everything in the oven and the warming closet, and a stick of wood in the stove to keep it warm.

Commentary: Cousin Lewis Garrett, known later to most as Nimrod, liked for you to ask the time when it was six o'clock, and it didn't matter to him if it was AM or PM, his answer was always: "It's straight up and down six o'clock."

That would be when the **air** hand was on the six and the minute hand was on twelve forming a straight line.

Airish

Meaning: Very cool but not freezing. This was the way my daddy described a cool, brisk autumn or spring morning.

Phrase in use: Better wear a jacket kids, it's a little **airish** out there this morning.

Are you taking medicine

Meaning: Are you on a schedule?

Phrase in use: Cleston says when he was a boy in grade school at Ozone and someone asked what time it was, or looked at their watch, another in the group would always ask, **"Are you taking medicine?"**

Commentary: Cleston's school was not more than ten miles from my school but I never heard that phrase until he said it to me just recently. The Ozone school and several other one-teacher schools in that area were consolidated in the late 1940s or very early 1950s into what became the Independence School. When Independence closed in the early 1980s, students that attended there were consolidated into Allons and Livingston schools.

A'tall

Meaning: A contraction using the words "at" and "all."

Phrase in use: Jessie asked, "Do you want the thigh or the pulley bone?" Came the reply from Stanpats, "It don't matter none **a'tall** jest so's it's chicken."

Commentary: Younger members of the family always wanted the pulley bone because as soon as we gnawed off all that delicious white meat, we'd call for someone to pull it with us; then, whoever got the short piece of the bone would have his wish come true. Oh, the fortunes I've gained and the young girls whose affections I've won after getting the short piece of the pulley bone.

Do you ever wonder what has happened to chicken bones? Restaurants now serve chicken strips, chicken nuggets, popcorn chicken, and chicken tenders and you never see a bone. It seems now there is a breed of boneless chickens. Wonder how they stood up and walked?

Ain't worth a plug nickel

Meaning: It's of very little value, whatever the item might be.

Phrase in use: Bill was asking fifty dollars for his old cow and everyone knew she wasn't worth **a plug nickel**, but Oscar went ahead and bought her anyway despite his friends trying to warn him about Bill's trading practices. The cow was already dry when the trade took place and never raised another calf. Poor Oscar never got a drop of milk or a calf from her and finally sold her for $7.

All'us

Meaning: Always.

Phrase in use: No matter how hard she tries to be on time, she's **all'us** late.

An ax to grind

Meaning: Getting revenge.

Phrase in use: Jasper has **an ax to grind** with Sid for stealing his dog.

Commentary: Even after all the years since the construction of Dale Hollow Dam, which began during WWII, many residents of the area who were forced to leave their homes and good farms still have **an ax to grind** with the U.S. Government because of that.

An old wid'der woman's farm

Meaning: A productive farmland that was worth much more than the colorful phrase would indicate.

Phrase in use: My son and I bought hay from Mr. Melton one winter and he had a farm for sale. When we inquired about it, his reply to us was: "It's just **an old wid'der woman's farm**" meaning, in actuality, it was a good farm.

And that's that

Meaning: That's the end of the matter and there's nothing more to be said about it.

Phrase in use: Ruby Ray always said **and that's that** when she finished a job or someone she trusted had completed a statement with which she firmly agreed.

Commentary: Ruby's favorite TV station was channel five in Nashville. Her favorite weatherman on that station was Ron Howes, and she watched him faithfully every day. Ruby would often say, "If Ron said it is going to snow, it will, **and that's that.**"

Anybody's dog that will hunt with him

Meaning: He'll buddy-up to anyone if it will give him an advantage.

Phrase in use: When we heard the judge was seen talking to his opponent's cousin, we weren't surprised at all because around election time he's just **anybody's dog that will hunt with him.**

Arr

Meaning: An arrow.

Phrase in use: In a contest they'd always watch to see who could shoot their **arr**s further. Those **arr**s were actually stickweeds shot from homemade bow n'arrs. That's what they called bows and arrows.

As long as Dick stayed in the army

Meaning: A comment heard when it wasn't expected that someone would be gone very long or that he would "stick it out."

Phrase in use: One might ask "How long do you expect Will to stay in Akron?" The answer, "About **as long as Dick stayed in the army.**"

Commentary: One might then wonder how long did Dick stay in the army? Well, he went in lighting his pipe and came out smoking it.

When thinking about "sticking it out," the author is reminded of the time Will went to Akron looking for work. He was being interviewed by one of the big rubber shops and was asked what sort of job he'd like to have. Will's reply was that he wanted one with the leastest work and the mostest pay. Needless to say, he didn't get the job and was soon hitchhiking south with two of his friends.

Will later related that they walked most of the 500 miles back home and their shoes were worn off their feet when they got back.

At herself/hisself

Meaning: Sane or cognizant.

Phrase in use: "Jessix is telling that Millie went off her rocker a few days ago and isn't back **at herself** yet." Reply, "That's correct, he is. But to tell the truth of the whole matter old Jessix never has been completely **at hisself,** and probably never will be."

Atter

Meaning: After.

Phrase in use: "Go on ahead and I'll be there **atter** awhile."

Axe

Meaning: Ask.

Phrase in use: "**Axe** your Momma if you can stay all night at my house." Her reply was usually, "You go ask your daddy and if he says it's all right, then it's all right with me." They often fudged a little by misleading Daddy to believe Momma had already given approval without restriction. It usually worked for the children.

B

Back an envelope

Meaning: To address an envelope. (They pronounced it EN-velope.)

Phrase in use: My hand is sore honey, will you please **back an envelope** for me?

Bad off

Meaning: In bad health or in dire financial straits.

Phrase in use: Paddlefoot has been **bad off** health-wise for years, but now he's **bad off** financially too.

Bald face lie

Meaning: A complete untruth with no effort to disguise — just an out-and-out lie.

Phrase in use: They are telling that the school teacher had an affair with one of her students, but it's not true. That's just another **bald face lie** they're spreading to try to get rid of her because she makes the children mind.

Band box

Meaning: Dressed in your Sunday best.

Phrase in use: A mother told her daughter she looked like she just stepped out of a **band box**, but what was a band box?

Commentary: The writer speculates it was the orchestra pit where the band sits to play during a stage presentation. They always dressed up for the performance.

Barefooted

Meaning: Wearing no shoes or socks.

Phrase in use: Mother never let us go **barefooted** until the first day of May. In the spring, we all went **barefooted**; however, our citified friends would always say "barefoot."

Commentary: Since it is easier to rhyme using the city folks' version of the word, I have used it that way in this poem I wrote about my boyhood. I can say it now, my sister and I fudged many times and went **barefooted** before the first day of May.

The Barefoot Days

Things have changed since the barefoot days,
people are the same, but they've changed their ways.

Mama cooked breakfast on a wood cook stove,
and we walked to school down an old dirt road.

Teacher kept order with a hick'ry stick,
and we learned to read, write, and 'rithmetic.

We carried our water from a deep cave spring,
and we washed our feet in a zinc wash pan.

Evenings were long and wouldn't you know,
the battery'd go dead on the old Philco.

Saturday at last, Oh! Day of joy,
there's a double feature, a Gene and a Roy.

Yes, things have changed since the barefoot days,
and I wouldn't go back to those quaint old ways.

But I like to recall those by-gone times,
and set my memories down in rhymes.

Be pur'ty

Meaning: Be on your best behavior. The writer heard this all during his childhood but never hears the expression now.

Phrase in use: It had nothing to do with looks, but rather how we behaved when we were out of our parents' sight. "Now you children be pur'ty and don't get in no trouble while I'm gone," Mother would caution.

Be smart

Meaning: Your, very, very best behavior.

Phrase in use: Most of the grannies and mamas said be smart in reference to good behavior. It had nothing to do with intelligence as one might think, but referred solely to a person's behavior. **Be smart** means exactly the same thing as "be pur'ty."

Beat around the bush

Meaning: Using many words without really saying anything. Somewhat the way many politicians are skilled at doing.

Phrase in use: Just come out and say it and don't **beat around the bush** about it. If you don't like the new preacher, just say so.

Bedfast

Meaning: Extremely sick and unable to get out of bed for a long period of time.

Phrase in use: Arnold's mother was **bedfast** for 20 years with arthritis before she was healed. After healing, she lived another 20 years or more and was never **bedfast** again up until her death.

Bein' haive yourselves

Meaning: Being on good behavior.

Phrase in use: Many be the times we were asked, "Are you young'uns **bein' haive** yourselves out there?" The answer was always the same, "Yes Mama we are." But we seldom were **bein' haive** ourselves. It was so hard to be good when our cousins came to stay all night.

Big as the side of a barn

Meaning: Extremely large.

Phrase in use: You remember how little Sally Mae used to be? Well, she ain't little any more, she as **big as the side of a barn** and getting bigger every day.

Biggity

Meaning: Acting snobbish or conceited.

Phrase in use: The Oldhams have been acting **biggity** since they traded their mule for that old car. Can you imagine how they'd act if they got a new car? But that won't happen; they don't have another mule to trade in.

Black as pitch, Dark as pitch, Pitch dark

Meaning: All meaning very dark or black.

Phrase in use: Jim and Rachel's youngest son Ethan reminded us of this old saying when he looked out the window one evening and stated, "It's as **black as pitch** out there." That happened right at **pitch dark**. Looks as if some of these old sayings are being passed down.

Black (or strong) as the Ace of Spades

Meaning: Extremely black or strong.

Phrase in use: Aunt Ove's coffee was always **black as the Ace of Spades**, while Cousin Betty would say, "This coffee is as **strong as the Ace of Spades**." A good comparison because the Ace of Spades is a strong card in most hands and will usually make the holder a winner.

Black as the Act of '40

Meaning: Very black.

Phrase in use: My mother always described something black as **black as the Act of '40** and I never heard it from anyone other than her. I don't know what the Act of '40 was but it must surely have been a bad Act. It was probably passed in 1840 because I had heard the expression prior to 1940.

Blackguard

Meaning: To curse strongly, taking God's name in vain. The British possibly used the word as a noun and referred to a person as a **Blackguard**.

Phrase in use: Old Tug cusses and **blackguards** something awful when he gets mad, and right in front of his young'uns. The British likely would call him a **Blackguard.**

Blame shore

Meaning: Absolutely!

Phrase in use: The Wilson brothers replied **blame shore** when asked if they had caught any fish lately.

Commentary: It was rumored around here that they had baited with dynamite. They say that's mighty good bait but you need to use it carefully, and carefully means when the Game Warden isn't on duty.

Bleeding like a stuck hog

Meaning: Bleeding profusely.

Phrase in use: When Bobbie wrecked his bicycle and cut his scalp, he was **bleeding like a stuck hog** when help arrived.

Commentary: This phrase came to be used during a time when pork and chicken were their main meat sources. The hogs were slaughtered by one hard blow with a nine pound sledge hammer right between the eyes or a shot to the same area with a .22 rifle.

Immediately a long, sharp butcher knife was stuck into the hog's neck and the jugular vein severed to "bleed" the animal. Thus came the saying, **bleeding like a stuck hog.**

Bless you out

Meaning: A good scolding or tongue lashing; a scolding of the worst kind, even worse than being rared on.

Phrase in use: If you ever dared to talk back to Mrs. Davis you could expect her to **bless you out** good. Then, if she didn't take a paddle to you, you could consider yourself extremely blest.

Blue old hen's chickens

Meaning: Something shady and not to be talked about.

Phrase in use: Better not bring up anything regarding the **blue old hen's chickens** because we're not allowed to discuss it. It's a secret matter or that's what Pat says.

Bolly foxin'

Meaning: Just joking or kidding.

Phrase in use: The last person remembered saying **bolly foxin** was the late Willie Beaty and that was several years ago. "Don't take it so hard, child, we were only **bolly foxin'** with you a little," he'd say.

Boot, To boot, Boot me

Meaning: The difference paid out in a trade.

Phrase in use: The first question asked after learning the age of the mule was, "How much **to boot** will you give me between this fine horse of mine and that old plug mule of yours?" The answer was usually, "Aw, I guess I'd **boot** you a two-dollar bill."

Commentary: About all the traders around these parts used these terms, especially those who traded horses and mules. You could, however, hear it used in a cow or hog trade.

Boyish bob

Meaning: The name of a certain hair style worn by the girls in the 1930s. Their hair was cut straight just below the ears with bangs in front, but without waves or curls as demonstrated in the picture above.

Phrase in use: Ronnie said that Jenny sure looked cute with her **boyish bob** but it did make her look kindly like a boy.

Brand spanking new

Meaning: Couldn't be any newer. If it's a car, it just rolled onto the showroom floor.

Phrase in use: He bought that car **brand spanking new** and just look at it now.

Brassiere

Meaning: The undergarment ladies and young girls used for support. Now everyone calls it a "bra."

Phrase in use: **Brassiere** was a bad word in earlier days and we boys were not allowed to say it in front of adults.

Bum steer

Meaning: Bad or misleading advice.

Phrase in use: Phil expected to make money on that last mule trade, but he was given **a bum steer** when the seller told him it was only three years old. Turned out the mule was at least 12 years old, had a limp in his hind leg, and was nearly blind in one eye. (Now that's what you call **a bum steer.**)

Bumfuzzled

Meaning: Confused or mixed up.

Phrase in use: That new teacher sure got **bumfuzzled** when she tried to explain "casting out nines."

Commentary: Casting out nines was a method of teaching long division to intermediate grades but this writer never tried to learn it. The conventional method always seemed less complicated.

Burn son

Meaning: Just another by-word that came from "dad burn."

Phrase in use: Sheldon said, **"Burn son**, we're going to be late if we hit that morning traffic."

Burning the wind

Meaning: Going real fast; so fast as to literally be **burning the wind.**

Phrase in use: They said that car was **burning the wind** when it passed, and no wonder, he was hauling a load of moonshine whiskey and the revenuers were right behind him; and, knowing the persistence of revenuers in their day, it was high time to be **burning the wind.**

Business is business and fuddling is fuddling

Meaning: If you're doing business do business, and if you're not doing business, you're fuddling.

Phrase in use: Pa Garrett's business motto was: **Business is business and fuddling is fuddling.**

Commentary: My Grandfather, Martin Garrett, used this phrase often. I was only 3 years old when he died, and have only one vague memory of him. I have heard this phrase used many times during my childhood and youth in reference to him. His name was always mentioned in conjunction with this saying.

Buss me

Meaning: Kiss me.

Phrase in use: "Here honey, **buss me** quick while nobody's looking," are words one might hear from young adults who were courting.

Commentary: In their day most courting or "sparking" was done at the girl's home in a room called the "parlor."

By crackey, By crackies

Meaning: Absolutely, it will happen.

Phrase in use: "**By crackey,** Joey! Will you fix me up with a date with Miss Lulu Belle?" The reply, "Be glad to, **by crackies,** and you all can go with my girlfriend and me to the show, that is, if Miss Lulu Belle will agree to go out with you."

By Nans

Meaning: A by-word only heard spoken by Grady and Rawhide.

Phrase in use: "**By nans,**" said Rawhide, "you catch another big fish on that jig and I'll tie one on my line just like it." And, sure enough he did.

By shockings

Meaning: Surprise!

Phrase in use: "**By shockings**! I never thought they'd land a man on the moon in my lifetime and I'm still not sure they have!" said Elzie.

By the skin of my teeth

Meaning: Just barely escaped.

Phrase in use: Job said, "I escaped **by the skin of my teeth**." He probably meant he had narrowly escaped death.

Commentary: May be the oldest "old saying" in this collection. It's from the book of Job 19:20, in the Holy Bible. It means "Just escaped death."

Got an old story?

_____

_____

_____

_____

_____

C

Can't turn off any work

Meaning: Can't get any work done. Means about opposite of what it sounds like.

Phrase in use: Since I got old, I just can't get much work done these days or, since I got old, I just **can't turn off any work** like I used to.

Cannipshun

Meaning: A tantrum or having a great big fit. The granddaddy of all fits.

Phrase in use: Aunt Jane and Uncle Frank's little boy had a real **cannipshun** when he found out he was starting to school, and I guess you would have had one too if you hadn't started to school until you were 10 years old.

Catty-cornered, Catty-wampus, Catty-gogglin

Meaning: Crooked, lopsided, or doesn't fit properly.

Phrase in use: The picture Kenny hung is so lopsided it's **catty-cornered**, **catty wampus**, and **catty goggling**, and will surely need to be rehung.

Charge it to the ground and let the rain settle it

Meaning: You're going to have to wait a while for your money and they understood that the phrase meant "you'll never get paid."

Phrase in use: Paul's neighbor did a little work for him and wouldn't say how much he was owed when the job was finished. Well, Paul told him he'd just **charge it to the ground and let rain settle it**, and lo and behold, the fellow came up with the amount owed him, right quick.

Cheap as gully dirt

Meaning: Of very little value.

Phrase in use: Alvin's got that car priced **cheap as gully dirt**. He's in trouble with the law again and he's having to sell it. He's turned out to be like the car price, **cheap as gully dirt.**

Commentary: Gully dirt is mostly red clay and is too poor to grow grass or even sassafras bushes and blackberry briars. The term was often used in evaluating property especially someone else's, but sometimes when referring to a person's character as in the above meaning.

Chicken one day and feathers the next

Meaning: Good one day and bad the next.

Phrase in use: Maisie was asked how she and Avery were doing and her reply was, "Well, you know how it is these days, **chicken one day and feathers the next.**"

Commentary: Better eat out when feathers come up. Don't you think, Avery?

Chomping at the bits

Meaning: Eager to go and to get on with it.

Phrase in use: Many farmers used this phrase seeing the mules **chomping at the bits** all day long.

Clear as a bell

Meaning: Heard clearly without any static or interference.

Phrase in use: The Grand Ole Opry came in **clear as a bell** on our new Truetone radio last Saturday night. When Roy Acuff sang "The Great Speckled Bird," it sounded like he was right there in the room with us.

Clouged in

Meaning: This quaint term was used only by my parents and I have no idea how it should be spelled. It meant a pact or plot against someone, and it may have come from the word "cloak" when used as a verb such as to "cloak" their evil deeds.

Phrase in use: The new sheriff was making a clean sweep of law breakers but a bunch of people across the river got **clouged in** together against him causing him to get beat in the very next election. They didn't like it when he busted up their stills and put them out of business for a while.

Commentary: Making illegal moonshine whiskey was an industry that flourished throughout the Appalachian and Ozark Mountains during the early 1900's, and was generally tolerated by most of the citizenry, especially if the moonshiner had a physical handicap. Often the sheriff just seemed to "look the other way." Those Federal Revenuers, however, were not so lenient.

Come by it honest

Meaning: Inherited. Not much was known about genes or genetics but that's exactly what this phrase refers to.

Phrase in use: "That boy has got a mean streak in him, and he'll probably end up in the pen before he's 21." Reply, "That's the truth, but he **come by it honest**. Don't you remember, his Pa died in the pen for killing his neighbor?"

Come to dinner, we don't have much but there's plenty such as 'tis

Meaning: There's not a wide variety of food available, but there's plenty of what they have such as beans, cornbread, 'taters, and side meat. When gardens come in you can add ripe tomatoes and roshn'ears.

Phrase in use: Florence invited the visitors, **"Come to dinner, we don't have much but there's plenty such as it 'tis."**

Come up

Meaning: A term used primarily in the south by those who drove mules. Northerners used the term "gitty up" instead.

Phrase in use: Come up Bob! **Come up** Frank! You lazy critters! We want to be home by dark.

Commentary: One simply said **come up** and the mule started. You could tell a lot about what the mule was thinking by observing his ears. If they flopped down, he was tired. When they stood straight up and twisted to the front a bit, he was startled, scared, or puzzled. If they were laid straight back, he was angry and it was best not to get behind him or you'd get kicked.

Coming around

Meaning: Getting better after a sick spell.

Phrase in use: Anytime you asked Maxie about his health, the answer was, "Oh, I'm **coming around**, jest **coming around**."

Consarn it

Meaning: Showing displeasure at something gone wrong.

Phrase in use: Cousin T.V. could often be heard saying to his dog, "**Consarn it,** Baldy, why don't you go out and tree a 'coon or a least an ole 'possum."

Cowed, Cowed down

Meaning: Humbled or embarrassed but having nothing to do with the Bovine species.

Phrase in use: The poor little puppy is **cowed** because he is lost. Sometimes one might day say that the puppy was **cowed down**.

Commentary: It seems that when a dog is **cowed** or **cowed down** he is embarrassed.

Crabby

Meaning: Fractious, peevish or short spoken, referring often to an older person or a teacher who was ill-natured.

Phrase in use: That old teacher is as **crabby** as she can be and getting crabbier every day.

Commentary: Miss Hillary could have been a great teacher if she hadn't been so all-fired **crabby.**

Crazy as a Bessie Bug

Meaning: Acting silly, inane, or crazy.

Phrase in use: One night Sophie went off her rocker and tore her house all to pieces. They're saying now she's **crazy as a Bessie Bug**.

Crooked as a dog's hind leg

Meaning: Sneaky and underhanded.

Phrase in use: "I'm not voting for Joe Sam again 'cause he turned out to be as **crooked as a dog's hind leg.**" Reply, "Yes, he's as crooked as the road down Cub Mountain to Alpine and that's mighty crooked."

Cuss a blue streak

Meaning: Cursing in a vile manner.

Phrase in use: James can **cuss a blue streak** when he gets mad enough, so you'd better stop up your ears when Mattie burns the biscuits.

Cut a shine

Meaning: Unruly, misbehaving or acting up.

Phrase in use: They say farmer Burgess really **cut a shine** when somebody stole the big watermelon he was saving for seeds. Nimrod's reply was, "Yeah I heard he really pitched a fit, but boy, wasn't that the sweetest watermelon you ever tasted? Oops!"

Cuttin' up

Meaning: Usually spoken of children who are teasing or playing around, not **cuttin' up** the winter firewood.

Phrase in use: You kids quit that **cuttin' up** or I'll wear you out! (Mama won't "wear" you when she goes outside, she can stay inside and still "wear you out.")

D

Dadgumit

Meaning: Aggravation.

Phrase in use: Dadgumit! It's supposed to rain all week during spring break.

Commentary: The Ledbetter sisters are old maids and they keep the party line tied up all the time talking to their friend in Georgia, **dadgumit**!

Dead level best

Meaning: To do one's absolute best in an endeavor.

Phrase in use: In a campaign promise years ago one candidate used this phrase: "If you will elect me, I'll do my **dead level best** to serve you honestly and efficiently."

Dead ringer

Meaning: To look exactly like someone else.

Phrase in use: "That new baby of the Smith's is a **dead ringer** for his pappy," stated the neighbor." Reply, "Yes he is, the poor little thing, but maybe he'll grow out of it."

Diapin

Meaning: Aw shucks or doggone.

Phrase in use: Diapin! Ann, I hope it doesn't rain before the boys get all the hay in the barn.

Commentary: This was Grandfather Garrett's by-word. I never heard another person use it unless they were quoting him. My Grandfather was a shrewd businessman who made his living in the timber business. Once he sold a tract of timber on the stump and the buyer was to cut all species of trees.

The price of logs went down and the buyer was losing money. Hickory trees were practically worthless at that time. He told Pa Garrett that he would just leave the hickory standing but my Grandfather refused and forced the man to pay him to keep the hickory.

Diddly squat

Meaning: Having little importance or value.

Phrase in use: Everyone knew Twylalee didn't care **diddly squat** about Roy J. and would surely break his little heart before she left town. Sure enough, she did! She left town and broke his little heart. It breaks my heart too. I just can't stand to see a six year old child cry that way.

Died out

Meaning: It or they expired.

Phrase in use: "Did you hear about Uncle Jake? He **died out** last week." Reply, "Why no, we didn't even know he was sick."

Digg'um

Meaning: Run as fast as you can.

Phrase in use: "Now **digg'um** boys or that old sow will catch you and eat you up," Uncle Tom would say, teasing us to see how fast we could run. He would laugh his head off as we raced to him.

Dilly-dally

Meaning: Extremely slow — wasting time.

Phrase in use: Now kids, don't **dilly dally** around this morning and go in late for school again!

Commentary: The Neal children walked from the Reed place in the Hunter Cove, across Palestine Mountain and on down to Cedar Grove. They didn't have to **dilly-dally** as they had a perfect excuse for being late because of the long distance they had to walk every day.

Disremembered

Meaning: A word seldom heard now but was frequently used in the past. It means forgotten or not remembered.

Phrase in use: Nancy **disremembered** that she was to bake a cake for the Saturday church picnic. She wouldn't even go because she was so embarrassed by having nothing to take.

Commentary: Read in a manuscript written by Mr. Charles Eldridge about the Bilbrey reunion: He stated that he **disremembered** many of the facts about the 1938 Bilbrey reunion, but remembered about the boy that was drownded that day.

Do a job

Meaning: Using the bathroom when it is necessary to sit down.

Phrase in use: Back in earlier times, most rural homes had no indoor plumbing, so they had to go to the outhouse or to the woods, when they needed to **do a job**.

Do to watch

Meaning: A person who can't be trusted.

Phrase in use: A new family moving into their neighborhood might evoke conversation such as this: "What do you think of that new feller that moved in here?" Reply, "Some folks seem to like him but I say he'll **do to watch**."

Dog tired

Meaning: Extremely exhausted.

Phrase in use: Finis and Finley walked the entire eight miles from town Saturday and were **dog tired** and soaking wet when they got home.

Doggone the doggone luck to the doggone devil

Meaning: Dang! Heck! Phooey! And all other by-words rolled into one phrase.

Phrase in use: Doggone the doggone luck to the doggone devil! That's what Daddy said when things went wrong, usually those pertaining to work or elections.

Commentary: One day they were trying to load a big log onto their truck and it rolled completely across the bed and down to the bottom of the holler. **"Doggone the doggone luck to the dog-**

gone devil, you boys let that big log roll clean off the truck and it'll take half a day to get it back up the hill and loaded again!" Daddy fumed. He didn't seem to remember that he was helping roll the log too.

Don't cut off your nose to spite your face

Meaning: A warning to one seeking revenge. You may hurt your cause rather than help it.

Phrase in use: Don't cut off your nose to spite your face trying to get back at another when they've hurt your feelings or wronged someone you love. A reminder: "Vengeance is mine sayeth the Lord."

Don't get your feathers ruffled

Meaning: A caution against getting angry or upset.

Phrase in use: I'm about to tell you what your kids have been doing but **don't get your feathers ruffled** up at me.

Commentary: The neighbor thought John needed to know what his kids got into while he was gone. John's reply was, "Doggone it! You're always the one to bring me bad news about my children!" Despite the request, John still **got his feathers ruffled**. This phrase is seldom heard anymore because there are not many chickens running around in every front yard to remind us to say it.

Don't fret your granny

Meaning: Don't let it worry you or anyone else.

Phrase in use: Don't fret your granny, Buster, we'll find your lost knife if it takes a week.

Don't look a gift horse in the mouth

Meaning: Be grateful, don't downplay a gift.

Phrase in use: I wouldn't grouse about the gift because there might never be another come your way. So the advice to be taken is **don't look a gift horse in the mouth.**

Commentary: Looking in the mouth of a horse or a mule to estimate its age might be proper if you're considering buying it, but insulting if it's a gift. So, take this old phrase at face value and don't, you know, look in his mouth.

Don't much care

Meaning: Very little concern about the matter, or it makes little difference one way or the other.

Phrase in use: J. C. went crazy over that new girl and he says he **don't much care** who knows it.

Commentary: Everyone allowed they'd be in for a wedding if things keep moving in the same direction and J. C. didn't get his eye on some other young lady. But remembering how fickle he is when it comes to the ladies, no one got their hopes too high.

Don't sugar-coat it

Meaning: Just tell the plain truth about the matter.

Phrase in use: When I was teaching and a student got into trouble I would always be easier in administrating the discipline if they just told me straight out, didn't lie to me, and didn't try to **sugar-coat it.**

Commentary: Teachers don't like tattletales because there are sometimes things you don't need to know, but they do appreciate those students who will discretely offer information when one has committed a serious infraction or as it is now called a "zero tolerance" offense.

Don't take no wooden nickels, Don't kill no dead snakes

Meaning: Don't be taken in or fooled.

Phase in use: **Don't kill no dead snakes** on your way home boys, we don't want you coming in here snakebit!

Don't that cock your pistol

Meaning: Surprise responses!

Phrase in use: They say Uncle Jay and Aunt Marge are getting married. **Don't that cock your pistol!**

Don't start in

Meaning: This is what they said when they were about to be rared on or scolded. It meant don't begin on me or **don't start in** on me.

Phrase in use: Velvet admitted to the teacher what she had done, and said to her parents, "**Don't start in** on me. I've already been punished for slapping Ed's face."

Don't you see

Meaning: Don't you understand?

Phrase in use: Clarence said, "We can swap work. I'll help you work tomorrow, **don't you see**, if you will help me the next day. It is remembered that Clarence would put an "H" in the phrase and it would sound like this, **"Don't 'che-shee."**

Doost bum'it

Meaning: Like dang or darn it, this phrase was used when things went wrong.

Phrase in use: Doost bum'it! That old cow is out again!

Down in the dumps

Meaning: Not meaning a junkyard tramp wandering through the rusty iron. This is a state of the mind such as "feeling low."

Phrase in use: When old George, my hound dog, went missing I was really **down in the dumps**.

Commentary: For a boy of only 10, I was deeply concerned and really **down in the dumps**. In the late afternoons I searched all over our farm whistling and calling for him to come to me but he never showed up again.

I was a middle-age man before it occurred to me what happened to old George. When the dog went missing, Uncle J.T. lived very near to us. He raised guineas and took great pride in the chicks they produced. He told Daddy that old George was catching and killing the guinea chicks and he had to be stopped.

I was warned to keep George at home, but one day he came to me with a dead chick in his mouth, which I quickly took and buried hoping he wouldn't do it again. Just a day or two later my dog was gone.

Many years passed before it dawned on me that my uncle had shot old George, but by that time, he and my parents had already passed away and no one else knew the answer to my suspicion. One thing is for sure, it took me a long time to figure it out.

Down in the mullygrubs

Meaning: Really feeling low or maybe near the point of depression.

Phrase in use: You sure are **down in the mullygrubs** today. What's wrong? Did your milk cow die?

Drama Queen

Meaning: A female who craves attention and excitement and acts out in any way to get both.

Phrase in use: Since she won that last beauty contest, Neva has become a real **Drama Queen.**

Commentary: The cliché **Drama Queen** is a relatively new term but **"Drama Queens"** have been in existence probably since the Garden of Eden; therefore, it is worthy to be included in this listing of by-words, etc., which reminds this writer of an incident that happened many years ago.

Old Aunt Dulcie had always been a person that would gain attention by exaggerating the details of the most minor incident to make you think it was about 10 times more serious than it really was.

This is an example of one such exaggeration. Her husband, Eddard, or as he was commonly known, Uncle Ed, was sick most of their married life, although no doctor near or far could ever diagnose anything seriously wrong with him. One cold winter morning Aunt Dulcie came huffing and puffing up the hill from the little cabin down below where they had kept house all their married life. Her face was red and she seemed frustrated and completely exhausted from the climb.

"What in the world is wrong, Aunt Dulcie?" her neighbor asked with great concern for the old woman's health.

"Ed's dead," she replied, speaking in a very low tone of voice without showing much emotion.

"Oh my!" cried the neighbor, "let me call in some friends and get you some help just as soon as possible. Are you sure he's dead?" she asked.

"Well nearly," came the reply. "He had a spell during the night but he didn't hardly die."

Come to find out, Uncle Eddard wasn't any worse off than he'd been for the last 25 years, and he lived on for several more years. That's why one can truthfully say that although the title **Drama Queen** may be new, Drama Queens have always been amongst us.

Dressed fit to kill

Meaning: Really dressed up. You could kill him and he'd look good enough to bury right then.

Phrase in use: We all thought young Russ was so dressed up for his date last night that if he died we could just bury him right then. You see, he was **dressed fit to kill.**

Dressed to the nines

Meaning: Dressed up similarly as being dressed fit to kill. Both meant you were very much in style.

Phrase in use: Betty had Shelvie **dressed to the nines** for her graduation party in Ohio.

Drownded

Meaning: Drowned.

Phrase in use: Over 150 people have **drownded** in Dale Hollow Lake since its impoundment and not one of them was wearing a life jacket. Sometimes the word was used in this manner: "A boy got **drownded** in Carter's Creek last week."

Drum up some business

Meaning: To stir up some business. This came from the word "drummer" (not the same as a percussionist but someone who worked as a salesman) and always referred to sales.

Phrase in use: Daddy told me the reason they were called "drummers" was because they were always trying to **drum up some business.**

Drunker'n a biled owl

Meaning: Totally inebriated.

Phrase in use: If you met J.J. in town on Saturday you could count on him being **drunker'n a biled owl**. Those more cultured would probably say that he was as drunk as a "boiled" owl but they shortened "boiled" to "biled."

Druther

Meaning: Rather

Phrase in use: Uncle Dumas said he'd **druther** live in Celiney than to live in California any day.

Duck soup

Meaning: Easy to do.

Phrase in use: It escapes me how **duck soup** would be easy but it was often used in this comparative manner. Could be **duck soup** is easy to eat, or maybe it was easy to prepare.

Dumb as an ox

Meaning: Stupid to the point of being unteachable such as a cow.

Phrase in use: Our old blind mule pretended to be **dumb as an ox** but he was just playing on his handicap to get out of work. His vision was 20/20 when he was turned toward the barn at quitting time, and he was always able to find the feed trough.

Dusty dark, Dusky dark

Meaning: The time after sunset and just before "good dark."

Phrase in use: When it started to get **dusty dark** or **dusky dark**, we had to be getting in home because we were already late doing up the night work.

Dyed in the wool

Meaning: An extra strong belief in one's politics or religion.

Phrase in use: Jockey Joe was a **dyed in the wool** Methodist and they say he was a strong Democrat too. There were those who believed he was a **dyed in the wool** horse thief also because of his unethical trading practices.

Commentary: Just hearing the name "Jockey Joe" conjures up a thought that he might do to watch in a trade. But, nonetheless, he had a clientele that wouldn't go anywhere else when they needed a mule or cow.

How did your family say it?

E

Eat and run

Meaning: In a rush and they'd be leaving the minute they finish eating.

Phrase in use: I hate to **eat and run** but I have to get home before dark.

Eat and started

Meaning: Justification for not eating because one was too shy or the place was just too dirty and nasty to suit them.

Phrase in use: "Come on boys, eat supper with us. We don't have much but there's plenty such as 'tis."

Being too shy they'd reply, "No thanks. We're full as ticks. We just **eat and started**." This means we left home as soon as we had eaten breakfast.

Eat your supper

Meaning: Admonishment to a youngster to eat some more. Encouraging request to eat more after one had finished and pushed back their plate.

Phrase in use: "Ah, **eat your supper**, you haven't eaten enough to keep a bird alive." The refusal, "I've had plenty — can't eat another bite."

Eats so much it makes him poor to pack it

Meaning: A reference to someone who was small and skinny yet was still a big eater.

Phrase in use: When I was a child I ate all the time and was still as skinny as a rail. Florence and Deller agreed, "Little Eddie **eats so much it makes him poor to pack it.**"

Commentary: Strange, when you're young and active you can eat anything you like and never gain a pound, but now every calorie seems to turn to fat, and sometimes just smelling good food may add a little weight.

Elt

Meaning: Surprise! Spoken when surprised by some word or deed. The word is not a contraction because only one word is involved. The intended word was "well" which was also used to show surprise.

Phrase in use: **Elt**! I didn't know the Vikings arrived here before Columbus!

Enough money to burn a wet mule

Meaning: Describing someone who has lots of money.

Phrase in use: Old Oliver is so well-off financially they say he has **enough money to burn a wet mule,** and that would require a big pile of money.

Every crow thinks his is the blackest

Meaning: Every mama thinks her child is the cutest and the smartest.

Phrase in use: "Have you seen baby Savannah lately? Why she's a dead ringer for little Shirley Temple." Response, "I guess so but then **every crow thinks his is the blackest.**"

Commentary: Most bird lovers hate crows but I like them. One year an old crow that visited our back yard had only one leg and the others protected him. He was always first to eat and three or four crows stood guard around him. They place sentinels in trees that sound the alarm when danger is near.

Ever'day clothes

Meaning: Clothes worn every day around the house and the opposite of "Sunday go to meeting clothes."

Phrase in use: First thing I'd do when I got home from school was change into my **ever'day clothes** and get ready to do up my night work such as, carrying in stove wood, feeding the chickens and hogs, and milking the cow.

Ever how many, Ever how long it takes

Meaning: Just as long as it takes. Whatever or however many it takes to pay the bill or finish the job.

Phrase in use: "Don't fret your granny son, we'll be here **ever how long it takes** to finish the job," stated Lewis.

Everybody and his brother

Meaning: Everyone.

Phrase in use: Everybody and his brother uses this expression and that explains the meaning of the phrase. Everybody!

Every tub has to sit on its own bottom

Meaning: Everyone is responsible for their own actions.

Phrase in use: "Looks like that young man is going to jail for a long time." Reply, "Well, it's bad but like they say, **every tub has to sit on its own bottom,** although sometimes it is unpleasant."

F

Far

Meaning: Burning flames or just plain fire.

Phrase in use: There's a huge **far** burning over on the other side of the ridge and the firefighters can't make any headway putting it out.

Fard

Meaning: Forehead.

Phrase in use: Everyone used to tease Cindy about the freckles on her **fard,** but she didn't mind at all. She knew they thought she was cute and soaked up their attention like a sponge.

Commentary: Some people who had high foreheads or receding hairlines were said to be **high-farded.** Seems that all men today are high-farded because most have no hair at all — they shave their heads.

Faster than lightning, Faster than greased lightning

Meaning: Extremely fast.

Phrase in use: One of the Ledbetter boys was **faster than lightning** but his little brother was **faster than greased lightning**.

Commentary: Just looking at the illustration reminds me of a very scary storm that hit our parts a while back — a storm that I will never forget because of the havoc it created.

Commentary: Our county was hit by an F-2 tornado last year, causing much devastation and wreaking havoc through one small community. By the grace of God, no one was killed or even seriously injured.

This brought back memories of a storm I was in way back in my childhood that sent a jolting electrical shock through my body, almost took the life of my cousin, and burned our barn to the ground. It was not a tornado, but a severe electrical storm such as no one in this area had ever seen.

The storm that roared through here on March 2, 2012, stirred old memories about the day I was…

...Lightning Struck

On Friday, August 3, 1945, I was 12 years old. That day, my cousins and I were very excited to be leaving the Cedar Grove School a little earlier than usual.

Another reason for our excitement was that it had been extremely dry for the past few weeks and, as usual in dry summers, we had to carry water for the hogs because our pond always dried up in the summer. The cattle and mules could be driven down the hill past our house and watered at a spring, but two pair of mules and several hogs were stabled in our old barn that contained about 40 wagonloads of loose hay that we had labored since spring to put in the barn to keep dry.

I had no brothers and only one sister but was richly blessed with first cousins, 10 on my daddy's side of the family, and 6 on my mother's side. Ten of these cousins were males and six were females. Except for about four of the older ones who had married or left home for other reasons, I was with these cousins, especially the boys, most of the time. They all lived near us in the Cedar Grove community.

On the above-mentioned date, a dark cloud began to form in the southwest and the wind started blowing steadily sometime during evening's recess. There was something ominous about this cloud and the teacher must have sensed that it was coming up a bad storm.

There was lightning almost continually as she dismissed school and sent us on our way home, with a warning to hurry so we could beat the rain. I remember that we didn't take the warning too seriously as we made our way up the gravel road toward my home near the old Celina highway.

As we came closer to the house, several of the students had already reached home or taken a short cut to the main highway. By now, the sky had turned a strange yellow color and was constantly aglow from the lightning, which was striking trees and fence posts all around where we were walking.

I guess I would have been very scared if not for the attitude of my older cousin, Finis Buck. He began to talk to the lightning after each strike. He would say, "Lightning strike that tree!" or, "Strike that fence post over there, but don't strike me!" This made me even more nervous because it was almost as if he was tempting God.

Now, as I think back on his strange actions, I believe he was using this flippant attitude to try to keep us calm. He was almost four years older than me and I viewed him as a hero. He was my idol. He knew more about cars and machinery at 15 years old than most experienced mechanics, and he could fix anything that needed fixing. He was always that way and is still very capable even at age 85.

Upon reaching my house, the cloud seemed to have "gone around" and up Mitchell's Creek as it often did in dry weather. After we had gobbled up all the food left from breakfast and dinner, and most likely what my mother had planned to have for supper, we noticed that another cloud was coming up, but this one was coming out of the East. We were disappointed because we seldom got rain from that direction.

As the dark clouds drew nearer, we soon saw that this storm was going to be much worse than the one that had just passed by. Thinking for sure we would get some rain this time, the four of us headed for the barn as fast as we could go to watch our pond fill up with water. We were elated because this meant a lot less time would have to be spent doing up the "night work." After all, Finis and I were planning to hitchhike into town that evening to watch a picture show at the Ritz Theater.

Just as we reached the shelter of the barn, the rain was pouring harder than I'd ever seen, and great streaks of lightning constantly illuminated the yellow sky. It was surely a strange looking time, but we were oblivious to the imminent danger presented by those long streaks of lightning that were, once again, dropping all around us.

Finis and I went to the side of the barn that faced the pond while Billy and Shelvie, Finis' younger brother and sister, began to play on a rope swing in the barn aisle. We had no fear at this time.

As we peered out two tiny windows in the side of the barn to watch the pond fill with water, I was holding on to the planks around the window and Finis was at the next opening. Our elbows were touching as the lightning continued to streak across the sky and to the ground.

Suddenly, I was stuck to the barn! My hands were drawn tightly and I could not turn loose. If you've ever experienced an electrical shock, you know the sensation I felt. Lightning had struck!

When I was finally loosed from my grip on the window, I saw Finis drop stiffly backwards to the barn floor. His tongue was sticking out between clinched teeth and his eyes rolled back in his head showing nothing but white. His lips were purple and I had no doubt that he was dead. The other two children were both crying. Somehow, I managed to stay calm and maintain my composure as I helped them through the barn gate and then we raced to the house.

Daddy was coming out the front door to check on us and I blurted out, "Lightning struck the barn and Finis is dead!" Daddy told me to go to our neighbor, Fate Ferrell, and ask him to come quickly and help out.

As I cut through the path by the bee gums to the road, I heard a terrible roar behind me. I stopped just long enough to look back and see that the barn was on fire and black smoke and flames were shooting 30 to 50 feet high. Those weathered old planks in that aged building and the many wagonloads of dry hay were all ablaze.

I reported to Fate that Finis was dead and he took off in a run toward our house, with me right behind. Suddenly he stopped, turned, and told me to stay at his house until he returned. I guess he thought that a 12 year old should not see more than I had already seen. I did exactly as I had been told because in those days you always obeyed an adult no matter who it was.

In the meantime, daddy had gone into the barn, carried Finis to a safe distance across the road, and laid him on the wet ground beside the corncrib. He then made his way back into the burning barn and opened all the stable doors where the mules and hogs were penned. Amazingly, they all escaped the fire and nothing was lost except the barn, hay, and a farm wagon. One of the mules did suffer some burns on his flank but not enough to keep him from working a few days later.

There were no telephones in our community at that time but that didn't keep the news from spreading like wildfire. Soon a steady stream of traffic lined old Mitchell's Creek Road and I could only pace back and forth across the Ferrell's front yard anxiously awaiting a word about Finis. I knew for sure that he was dead but I guess I needed to hear someone else say it.

Finally, after what seemed like an eternity, Fate returned. I saw him coming and ran to meet him as he approached his house. "How about Finis?" I asked anxiously, feeling sure in my heart that he was dead. Fate responded by saying that he was going to be all right. He said that he had just come-to after being unconscious for nearly three hours and that he was very sick and vomiting but would surely live and not die now.

My response was, "Don't you lie to me, Fate Ferrell!" as I burst into tears. I still couldn't believe that my cousin was alive. I thought it must be a lie. I don't remember how long I cried or how long it took me to realize that Finis was not dead. Words can never describe the feeling of relief that overwhelmed me.

We later learned that a neighbor, B. Ferrell, had just bought a new car. When he saw the situation, he tied the horn rim down and headed for town to get old Dr. Capps. Running wide open somewhere near Allons, he lost control and totaled his new car and almost killed himself in his effort to get help.

Dr. Capps finally did arrive and spent the night with Finis just to make sure there were no after-effects from the shock. He always said that the fact that Finis was laid on the wet ground was what saved his life. He stated that the cold, wet ground somehow alleviated the shock in his body.

I was so terrified of storms after that, that for years every night before I went to bed, I'd go outside and search the skies. If I saw even one little cloud, I'd lay awake all night worrying that it might come another storm. Many nights, I never slept a wink.

Editor's Note: Three other schools in the area also experienced similar situations to ours at Cedar Grove. Students at Independence, Palestine, and Ozone also suffered shock and burns from lightning strikes, but amazingly, although some were badly burned, no one was killed.

Favors

Meaning: To look like or resemble someone else.

Phrase in use: Some think little Ted **favors** his daddy, and he does a little, but others think he **favors** his mother's people some too.

Commentary: It has been said that everyone has a "double" somewhere in the world and it could be true; however, that theory has never been proven.

Feeling their oats

Meaning: Spirited and frolicking and often spoken of young mules when they were playful and feeling cocky. Similarly used to describe children as well.

Phrase in use: When the mules were turned out of the barn, they ran all over the pasture kicking and jumping because they were really **feeling their oats.**

Commentary: A recent edition of the *Herald Citizen*, a newspaper published in Cookeville, Tennessee, cited a statistic from a 1939 edition reading as follows:

> The Old gray mare ain't what she used to be. There were 832,000 mules and horses in the state two years ago (1937) and that figure has dropped by 400,000 since then. That's the word from a report in this week's edition from the UT Extension Service. Increased mechanism in farming and a two years old drought was blamed for the decrease.

With the interest in the walking horse industry one might wonder what the equestrian population is today.

Fell off

Meaning: An extreme weight loss often spoken in their day referring to someone who has lost weight, not someone who fell off a cliff, tower, or a high bridge.

Phrase in use: Betsy said, "She's **fell off** a lot since the last time I saw her." Guy added, "Yeah, she used to be a big, flashy woman."

Fidgerolly

Meaning: Lazy.

Phrase in use: "What are you doing today, Willie?" He replied, "Ah, just **Fidgerollying** around and not doing a thing."

Commentary: Usage is attributed to the late Willie Beaty and his brother-in-law Wilbur C. Smith who are remembered using the term. The phrase reportedly originated in Hogeye Country and was the name of a family that once lived there. Evidently they did not work and just laid around all day long.

Fine as fiddle dust

Meaning: Very fine, not coarse at all.

Phrase in use: Coley said, "That meal may be fine enough Uncle L. Why, it's already as **fine as fiddle dust.**"

Commentary: So what is fiddle dust? It's the fine dust that accumulates on a fiddle that has collected as the rosin from the bow falls onto the instrument while being played. It looks like a very fine white powder and "fiddle dust" would accurately describe it.

Another oddity, many fiddlers even today, try to find a set of rattlers from a rattlesnake to drop through the "F" holes into the fiddle claiming that keeps spiders away. (You don't want spiders in your fiddle.)

Fine as frog hair

Meaning: Something rare or maybe in abundance, but very fine or thin in shape or size.

Phrase in use: Wid'der Brown remarked about how fine and silky little Julie's long, blond hair looked after being washed with lye soap. She reckoned it looked as **fine as frog hair.**

Fit

Meaning: Used as the past tense of the verb fight instead of "fought."

Phrase in use: Two of them big boys got in a fight at Timothy last week and **fit** all over the school grounds before the teacher could stop them.

Fits like a sock on a chicken

Meaning: Something fits or works exceedingly well.

Phrase in use: Jim's homemade shirt **fits like a sock on a chicken.**

Fits, Fitified

Meaning: Having spells such as fits or seizures.

Phrase in use: People used to have **fits** or spells and were often referred to as **fitified.** Those fits could have been the results of epilepsy.

Flares

Meaning: Flowers. They made a one-syllable word out of a two-syllable one.

Phrase in use: Those are pretty **flares** you planted on Ma's grave.

Flashy

Meaning: Not shiny or glittery, but rather being obese with lots of flesh.

Phrase in use: She used to be small but now she's a big, **flashy** woman.

Flat as a flitter

Meaning: Very flat.

Phrase in use: They said **flat as a flitter** when referring to something that was very thin. Others would say "fritter" instead of **flitter**. Supposedly fritter would have been the correct word to use relating to flatness. One might be reminded of butterflies or tiny birds when using the word "flitter" but nonetheless, that's what they said.

Flat as a pancake

Meaning: Thin with no fluff at all.

Phrase in use: The tire on the old car was as **flat as a pancake**. Interestingly, flat tires along the highways are not seen often these days probably because of improvements that have been made in manufacturing tires. Another reason is that most of the population is better off financially now than they were back then and can buy new tires before they are completely worn out. (No more "bald" tires.)

Flippin'

Meaning: Aggravating.

Phrase in use: That **flippin'** car won't start a'tall in cold weather.

Flop eared as a mule

Meaning: A reference about a person whose ears were floppy or too large.

Phrase in use: That poor boy of Delbert and Anne's is as **flop eared as a mule.** He looks awfully homely to me but the girls all seem to think he is cute.

Fool self

Meaning: Acting foolishly without using good judgment. Taking risks that could be dangerous.

Phrase in use: If young Will doesn't stop driving so fast in that old car he just traded for he's liable to wreck and kill his **fool self.**

Foot take it, Foot fire, Foot fired fool

Meaning: Response to an aggravation.

Phrase in use: Foot take it we're having liver and onions for supper again tonight and I gag just thinking about it.

Commentary: June carter, of the famous Carter Family, was overheard using this expression on the Grand Ole' Opry: "I'll knock the **foot fired fool** out of you!" She was usually addressing her counterpart, Rod Brassfield during their comedy routine. **Foot take it** and **foot fire** were often exclaimed when something went wrong.

For me to know and you to find out

Meaning: A smart-aleck answer given to someone prying or being nosey about something private.

Phrase in use: Don't ask me again who I'm taking to the pie supper. That's **for me to know and you to find out.**

Commentary: The author is reminded of a particular pie supper and still wonders what happened to the pies the winning bidder, "Tapper" Tom purchased.

"Tapper" Tom was a talented man who could do about anything he was called upon to do. A new talent was discovered one Saturday night in 1945. Tom had just been mustered out of the Army and had money in his pockets. When Tom had money, everyone knew about it. He made sure of that.

A pie supper was held at the Cedar Grove School to raise funds for school supplies. A large crowd showed up and 21 young ladies had each brought a pie. The custom was that each pie was auctioned and the high bidder ate the pie with the girl who had brought it; then, he was allowed to walk her home.

One problem was soon discovered — there was no one to auction the pies. Well, it seems that this was not a problem because "Tapper" Tom stepped right up and volunteered to be the auctioneer. Once again, he was like many of the Old Testament Kings, his heart was merry from drink.

The newly appointed auctioneer opened the bid on every pie at 50 cents. He bought 20 of the 21 pies and allowed Clyde (Cicero) Garrett to buy number 21. It's remembered that Clyde only had to pay a quarter for his pie.

One might imagine the ladies were a little disappointed because "Tapper" Tom could not possibly walk them all home. But then, maybe "relieved" would be a better choice of words knowing "Tapper" Tom as they did.

77

Foun't, Foul'nd

Meaning: Found.

Phrase in use: Johnny said he **foun't** the knife that he lost last year and Lonnie said he was sure glad he had **foul'nd** it.

Fractious

Meaning: Unruly, peevish, and crabby or describing a person who is hateful.

Phrase in use: Somebody remarked that Wheeler has been awfully **fractious** since he's been sick. His wife said not just since he's been sick, he's always been **fractious,** hateful, and crabby with her.

Friday week

Meaning: One week from Friday. Common in past usage but finds limited use today.

Phrase in use: He didn't know that **Friday week** meant a week from Friday.

Commentary: This conversation took place in Mrs. Carlen's classroom recently when the question came up about when the next math test was to be given. Mrs. Carlen's reply was, "**Friday week.**" The student asked, "What in the world does that mean?"

"If you can't figure that out by now, you don't need to know any-way," replied Mrs. Carlen.

From off from here

Meaning: Strangers. They're from somewhere else.

Phrase in use: "Did you see that load of strangers that stopped off down at the store yesterday?"

"Yeah, they're **from off from here** somewhere and they were driving that odd looking car that said Marathon Motor Works of Nashville. Never seen one of them around here before."

Fur

Meaning: For. Al Capp, the creator of Lil' Abner, spelled it "fer."

Phrase in use: One young man said to another, "What'd you do that **fur**?" Their answer, "Cat **fur** to make you a pair of kitten britches." A cat in britches?

Fur

Meaning: Pronounced and spelled the same as fur of an animal but used to express distance, meaning "far."

Phrase in use: "We're going to California, would you like to go?" "No, it's too **fur** away from home to suit me."

G

Gad blame

Meaning: Disgust.

Phrase in use: "**Gad blame** it, that hound's lost again!"

Gad dum'it

Meaning: Dad gum'it! There were those who just reversed the first letters of this phrase.

Phrase in use: "Gad dum'it! The beans will have to be replanted because of the late freeze!" snorted Marcia.

Gag a maggot

Meaning: Something sickening and odious such as kyarn or as bad as the smell of a dead 'possum's carcass.

Phrase in use: "Did you smell Hank's feet when he took off his shoes last night? The odor was strong enough to **gag a maggot**." Replied Bill, "Smelled just like kyarn to me."

Commentary: A famous country music entertainer, whose name won't be mentioned here, had feet that stank so badly everyone left the room when he removed his boots.

Gangly

Meaning: A long, tall teenager who is in a growth spurt and seems to be all arms and legs; however, this word is seldom used to describe a girl. It's probably because they're not as awkward as boys are at that age.

Phrase in use: That tall, **gangly** boy down the road will make a great ball player if he ever stops growing.

Commentary: There's a boy in the sixth grade who is already six feet tall and still growing. If he keeps growing at the same rate the pros will be recruiting him before he enrolls in high school. You can most likely look for him in the big arenas and on the wide screen if he can establish some coordination.

Gassing

Meaning: Kidding or joking.

Phrase in use: Don't get mad son, they're just **gassing** with you a little bit. They're trying to get your goat.

Gee-haw

Meaning: How well two people get along.

Phrase in use: Me and Sam don't **gee-haw** too well these days after he never paid back the two dollars I loaned him to go to the circus a few months back.

Commentary: To the mules **gee** meant turn right and **haw** meant turn left. The mention of mules brings to mind a poem this writer penned for a friend. It follows:

The Coupling Pole

The old farm wagon rumbled down the road, with a tow-headed boy on the coupling pole, the lead mule's mean and known for baulking, 'twas a rough old ride but it sure beat walking.

The old farm wagon's hauled many a load, with a tow-headed boy on the coupling pole, 'twas the family ride to church on Sunday, and back in the hay field early on Monday.

On the old farm wagon time's taken its toll, no tow-headed boy on the coupling pole, it now sits idle in a run-down shed with its broken spokes and its empty bed.

The tow-headed boy is all grown up, he now drives a shiny, new truck, for a twist of fate has changed the rules in a fancy trailer he pulls the mules, from town to town and show to show, and nobody rides on the coupling pole.

Get after

Meaning: To scold or reprimand someone.

Phrase in use: "Pappy, you need to **get after** them kids or they're going to get completely out of hand." (They already are! The little brats!)

Get your readies on

Meaning: Get ready now!

Phrase in use: Daddy always said this to his children and to any other young person who might be present, when they were preparing for a job. "**Get your readies on**, we have to leave here in fifteen minutes."

Getting up a case

Meaning: The beginning of a romance.

Phrase in use: Jack and Jill are really **getting up a case** and they'll probably jump the broom before summer's end.

Give him an inch and he'll take a mile

Meaning: Give someone a little and they'll want more the next time.

Phrase in use: They extended his rent payments for six months and he didn't have to pay a penny. Yet, he had the gall to ask to stay another month for free, perfectly demonstrating this old phrase, **give him an inch and he'll take a mile.**

Give it a lick and a promise

Meaning: Do it quickly even if it's only half done.

Phrase in use: The children were supposed to give the garage a good cleaning Saturday but they got in a hurry and only **gave it a lick and a promise**. That will probably result in their allowances being withheld.

Give me some sugar

Meaning: Give me a little kiss.

Phrase in use: "Come here children and **give me some sugar** before you leave," begged Grandad.

Gob smacked

Meaning: Shock or surprise. This is an old Scottish word from Rachel who was born and reared in Scotland.

85

Phrase in use: Frank was **gob smacked** when he finally saw a real, live Leprechaun, or so he said. But those who know him well tend to doubt his story. Those Leprechauns are almost extinct now and difficult to spot, and Frank is near-sighted.

Going to town

Meaning: Moving fast in some endeavor.

Phrase in use: They're really **going to town** on that new house they're puttin' up.

Going in a long trot

Meaning: Keeping very busy and never having a free moment.

Phrase in use: Granny hasn't had time to do her spring-cleaning. She's **going in a long trot** all the time and she's going to wear herself plum out before she's 100 if she doesn't slow down.

Going together

Meaning: Someone who is seriously dating or courting.

Phrase in use: I hear tell Sally and Bill are still **going together** and it looks like they may get married soon if they don't break up.

Gollywhopper

Meaning: Exceedingly large or extra big.

Phrase in use: Did you hear about the fish they caught last week that got away? Boy! They said it was a **gollywhopper!** But isn't it strange they caught it but it got away.

Good old common, bay horse sense

Meaning: Someone just plain sensible in making decisions whether it be in business, church matters, romance, or just common everyday living. Most of the old timers living in their day firmly believed that this kind of sense was better than any learning that came from going to school or reading books. That may be the reason they placed a low emphasis on education.

Phrase in use: Make no mistake about it, young Malcolm is loaded with **good old common, bay horse sense**. He proved that when he outsmarted that lawyer on the town square a few days ago.

Got up on the wrong side of the bed

Meaning: In a bad mood.

Phrase in use: What's the matter with you young'uns this morning? Bet you **got up on the wrong side of the bed.**

Grab a cow tail and hang on

Meaning: Seeking a means of security in finding the way home in the dark.

Phrase in use: The use of the phrase is best explained by examining its origin. While the expression is upwards of 80 years old, it can be traced back to the person who first said it. Now it is commonly spoken by that family and by others who know them.

Agnes Moore is around 95 years old and resides in Fayette County, Tennessee. She still plants an "upper" and "lower" garden every year and generously shares her produce with neighbors, friends, and her church family.

The phrase **grab a cow tail and hang on** originated when she and her brother had the daily chore of bringing the cows back to the barn after they had grazed all day in the fields below a slough (pronounced slu) of water that they crossed going to graze and returning in the late evening.

On one particular day, the cows had wandered further than usual and the Moore children couldn't find the bell cow who would lead the others back. The bell cow was the leader or boss of the herd and was fitted with a cowbell around her neck which made it easy to locate the herd when they roamed too far away. All they had to do was find her and turn her toward the barn, then the other cows would follow.

They were running late on this day, and by the time they got started back it was completely dark. Agnes wondered to herself how they would get safely across the slough in the dark, knowing it was teeming with leeches, snapping turtles, and water moccasins. "How will we ever cross the slough in the dark?" she cried aloud.

Her brother quickly answered, **"Grab a cow tail and hang on."**

They both did exactly that and the bell cow did her job, thus a new saying was born. It's anticipated that the Moore family has used the phrase during many crises over the years.

Grin and bear it

Meaning: Make the best of a bad thing. This is often the best thing to do.

Phrase in use: You may not like what's happening or whatever situation you may find yourself in, but there's nothing that can be done about it so you'll just have to **grin and bear it.**

Gumption

Meaning: No desire to work.

Phrase in use: The Fidgerollys were often discussed by the old timers around Bethsaida. Some said they didn't have a bit of **gumption**.

Commentary: Google shows only one Fidgerolly and that's Eliza Fidgerolly Smith of Monroe in Overton County, Tennessee. This very well may be the same person as mentioned previously in Section (F) above. The origin of this odd name is unknown to folks living around here.

Hain't, Haint

Meaning: Denying it as being so, meaning "ain't." Also used to identify a ghost or spook, "haint." This was their version of "haunt."

Phrase in use: "We thought we saw a **haint** down at the old vacant house near Raven Bluff." Come the reply, "That **hain't** no **haint** down there, that's a bunch of moonshiners scaring everybody away so they don't get caught."

Half-cocked

Meaning: Unprepared and not completely ready for the task whatever it may be.

Phrase in use: Lee went off **half-cocked** when he pulled his boat all the way to the lake before discovering he had forgotten to load his fishing equipment and bait.

Commentary: The ten virgins in the Bible offer a perfect illustration of the meaning of this phrase; or, five of them do — the five foolish ones who failed to trim their lamps and fill them with oil. They went off **half-cocked**.

Half-shot

Meaning: Not completely drunk, just somewhat inebriated.

Phrase in use: Jim Bob went to town early Saturday morning and came home about half-shot, but that's no surprise. Here lately he's about **half-shot** about all of the time.

Ham of meat

Meaning: A ham.

Phrase in use: When *they said it their way* they said a **ham of meat**.

Commentary: Back in the day there was a time when the Garretts, down to their last ham of meat, were desperately trying to get closer to hog-killing time without cutting their last ham. But one day Martin's craving for ham meat overtook his better judgment and he told Ann to go to the smokehouse and slice a slab of that last ham and fry it for breakfast.

Aunt Ann, as most of the neighbors called her, willingly obliged and headed for the smokehouse with a sharp butcher knife. She was back in a surprisingly short time with some alarming news. The last ham was gone! Someone had stolen it!

Try as they might they couldn't come up with one single clue or a suspect. But Uncle Martin, as he was called by most everyone in the community, had a plan…

…To Catch a Thief

It was really a simple plan but it proved to be very effective. You see, this was during the time when the Garretts ran a general store that housed the Grey City Post Office. This resulted in several people coming and going during the course of a day.

"Here's what we'll do," stated Martin. "We won't say a word to anyone about the theft, not one single soul." This was somewhat of a reversal of roles for the couple because Ann was usually the one who came up with the clever ideas. However, this time it was Martin who was a step ahead of her.

Again, he cautioned her not to tell a single person, not even a member of their own family. They both agreed to just wait and see what would happen, even though Ann was somewhat skeptical of the plan. There was not much they could do, since the thief had left no clues at all that would lead to his identity.

Many weeks passed and hog killing time came and went by, when one day Martin happened to be in the store alone. In walked a neighbor and made a small purchase or two and was just leaving the store. As he reached the door, he turned and asked, "Say, Martin, I was just wondering, did you ever find out who stole your ham?"

"Why, yes! Yes, we did!" Martin quickly replied. "We just found out."

Neither Ann nor Martin had ever uttered a word to anyone about the missing ham so this had to be the low-down culprit who had stooped to stealing. The man quickly exited the store, probably suspecting that he had said too much and that he had been found out. The identity of the man was never revealed during the many times this story was told down through the generations.

Happy as larks

Meaning: Joyful, without a care.

Phrase in use: My wife Peg's mother, Vallie (Padgett) Robbins wrote on the back of a picture of her children, Peggy, Patsy, Ted and Shelton: "They're as **happy as larks."** Isn't that just about as happy as a mother can be, seeing her children as **happy as larks?**

He needs to sweep off his own back step before he starts sweeping mine

Meaning: Response to a person who is reported to have made derogatory remarks about another person or their children.

Phrase in use: Old Backus has been saying awful things about our children, and **he needs to sweep off his own back step**

before he starts sweeping mine! He's going to need a big broom when he sweeps his own back step.

He ought to be cowhided

Meaning: Someone having done something really bad and should be punished severely.

Phrase in use: Al has been on a drunk six weeks and now he's in jail again, leaving his wife and hungry children at home penniless. Why! **He ought to be cowhided!**

He'd fight a buzz saw

Meaning: Brave enough to fight against any odds.

Phrase in use: Little Billy was not afraid of anyone and it was often said **he'd fight a buzz saw.**

He'd steal the nickels off a dead man's eyes

Meaning: A thief that would steal anything from anyone, even the dead.

Phrase in use: Never trust him, **he'd steal the nickels off a dead man's eyes.**

Commentary: Mother and Daddy said this in reference to a person who would steal anything he could get his hands on. The saying probably originated back in the days when most country people buried their own dead because there were few undertakers and the cost of a funeral would have been too expensive for poor, country folks to afford.

They said when a person died in those days the corpse was immediately "laid out." That means the dead body was placed in a prone position on his back, his mouth was closed with a kerchief bound around his chin and tied tightly at the top of his head. The eyelids were forced shut and nickels or sometimes quarters were then placed on top of the eyelids to prevent them from opening when rigor mortis set in.

He'd tell a lie when the truth would suit better

Meaning: He's an habitual liar, and the truth is not in him.

Phrase in use: Don't believe anything he says. Everyone knows **he'd tell a lie when the truth would suit better.**

He'll have to lick his calf over

Meaning: You didn't get it right the first time and will have to do the entire project again.

Phrase in use: Paul says his new roof is already leaking and that roofer, **he'll have to lick his calf over.**

Help a plenty

Meaning: Having all the help needed for a job.

Phrase in use: Carl did all the work himself and said he had **help a plenty**. When asked who had helped him complete the project, he replied, "Just we three, me, myself, and I."

Commentary: W.C. Smith told this writer that his father-in-law, Johnny Beaty hired a friend, Carl Gilpatrick, to build a barn for him. When the barn was completed and Carl was paid for his work, someone asked Johnny if they had a contract for the labor. He replied that you don't need a contract when two honest men shake hands on a deal.

This was the Carl Gilpatrick who served as Overton County Trustee and was the first public official to put the county's money in an interest-bearing account. This was a very popular maneuver and the people appreciated it.

He made his own bed, now he'll just have to sleep in it

Meaning: He brought the trouble on himself, now he'll just have to bear the consequences.

Phrase in use: Jimmy says he's sorry for the way he treated Julie and he'd give anything if she would come back, but **he made his own bed, now he'll just have to sleep in it.**

Head fo'most

Meaning: Plunging or falling headfirst or head foremost.

Phrase in use: The boy fell off the roof head **fo'most** and landed in the rain barrel or he would have probably broken his neck.

Heah

Meaning: Here!

Phrase in use: Heah! Puppy! **Heah! Heah**! This is the way "here" was pronounced when they called the dogs. Grandpa Jones of WSM's Grand Ole' Opry sang, "Heah Rattler! Heah! Heah!!" in his song by the same title calling his dog, Rattler.

Hear tell

Meaning: The news had been heard.

Phrase in use: "I **hear tell** that Lonzo is going to marry that rich old wid'der woman he has been sparking. Did you ever **hear tell** of such? Why, she's 25 years older than he is." Reply, "But, she's rich."

Heavens

Meaning: Disgust or aggravation.

Phrase in use: "**Heavens**, young Hall, did you stop up my fox horn again?" asked Walter.

Commentary: Stopping up a fox hunter's horn was a common prank when they enjoyed this sport so much, but the fox was never caught — just chased. The sport came from hearing each hound bay and having bragging rights about whose dog was in the lead.

He'd turn over in his grave

Meaning: The deceased wouldn't like what's going on now if he could know about it.

Phrase in use: We all allowed old man Palmer would have a fit if he knew how his widow is carrying on since his death. I guess **he'd turn over in his grave** if he did.

Het, Het up

Meaning: Used by the older folks in the community, it referred to someone getting mad and was used as the past tense of "heat."

Phrase in use: Sister Brown said, "Brother Smith got all **het up** preaching his sermon last Sunday." "Well I don't wonder! The temperature was up over 100 degrees and he preached nigh on two hours!" replied Deacon Ellerge.

Commentary: It their day there were no air conditioned churches in rural areas and few in the cities. Their "air conditioning" came from fans provided by local funeral homes and church was held in the local schoolhouse.

Hick'ry withe

Meaning: A long switch cut from a hickory tree and used for striping the legs of unruly children.

Phrase in use: You kids behave or I'll use a **hick'ry withe** on you.

Commentary: There's a settlement between Oakland, Tennessee and Memphis named **Hickory Withe** that is reminiscent of the times they have been exposed to a **hick'ry withe** applied freely to the backside between the shoulders and shoe heels.

High as a cat's back

Meaning: Way up! Usually referring to taxes or gasoline prices.

Phrase in use: Taxes in this country are as **high as a cat's back** now and going higher yearly.

High falutin'

Meaning: Uppity, egotistical, and snobby.

Phrase in use: Millie got to be **high falutin'** after marrying that millionaire.

High tailing it out'a here

Meaning: Leaving here in a hurry.

Phrase in use: They were last seen **high tailing it out'a here** headed home.

Highway robbery

Meaning: Price gouging.

Phrase in use: Gasoline is $3 per gallon and going higher by the day, and that's just plain **highway robbery.**

Hissy fit

Meaning: Throwing a big fit, just about the same as a spazomotic.

Phrase in use: Wilbur's student said, "Mr. Smith you just had a spazomotic yesterday, didn't you?" He could have said **hissy fit** and it would have meant the same. Judge Judy, the TV judge, says **hissy fit** often. Says she has one now and then.

Hitch in my gitty up, Catch in my gitty up

Meaning: Something has gone wrong.

Phrase in use: "Hold on boys, there's a **hitch in my gitty up** and you'll have to wait till it's fixed," said Gary. "Well heck! I've got a **catch in my gitty up!**" exclaimed Donald. Looks like those Ledbetter boys will never get where they're going.

Hit the hay

Meaning: Go to bed. Probably came from the straw tick mattresses they used on their beds after the wheat had been threshed.

Phrase in use: Go wash your feet kids, it's time to **hit the hay**. You'll sleep soundly tonight on those fresh straw ticks.

Hog wild, Hog wild and pig crazy

Meaning: Someone who had done something really foolish or silly.

Phrase in use: That boy's gone **hot wild** over the red haired girl, and if you ask me he's **hog wild and pig crazy** over her.

Commentary: **Hog wild and pig crazy** was probably the crazier of the two.

Hold your horses, Hold your 'tater'

Meaning: Don't get in a rush, just practice a little patience. Both meant exactly the same.

Phrase in use: "Just **hold your horses** a minute, I'm almost ready to go." Sometimes it was, **"Hold your 'tater**, I'm on my way!"**

Commentary: They didn't dare tell Mama to **hold your 'tater**. She was the one who always did the telling.

Hollerin' distance

Meaning: The distance from which another could hear you when you hollered or yelled loudly.

Phrase in use: Communication between the two friends was easy because they were within **hollerin' distance** of each other.

Commentary: In their day, Booze Mayberry said that when he was young Void Maynord would walk out to the edge of the hill and holler down to him to see if he wanted to go 'coon hunting. They lived a great distance apart and there were no telephones back then. The Maynords lived on top of a hill and the Mayberrys lived down below in the valley. They were able to communicate because they were within **hollerin' distance** of each other. Wonder how that would work today?

Hope up

Meaning: Used in reference to a sick person and that there was some hope that he might live.

Phrase in use: "How's Aunt Maude this morning?" "Well she was awful sick yesterday but her fever broke sometime in the night and we're all **hope up** about her today."

Hotter'n a red hot poker

Meaning: Really hot as related to a red-hot poker that stood by the fireplaces in their homes.

Phrase in use: That cup of coffee that the waitress poured was **hotter'n a red-hot poker.**

Commentary: The waitress became extremely angry when the customer claimed that his coffee had been reheated; however, she cooled off quicker than the cup of coffee when he jokingly explained that it could not possibly have been that hot without being heated twice. But it all ended well when he gave her a generous tip. Nellie exclaimed that no one had ever given her a one dollar tip before and that she hopes that customer returns to her table often.

I

I ain't going to hell for a nickel

Meaning: I'm telling the truth.

Phrase in use: Said the preacher, "I'm telling it straight, **I ain't going to hell for a nickel.**"

I can't do everything and go to mill too

Meaning: Expressing the feeling that one is being overworked.

Phrase in use: "When you finish carrying in the wood, run out to the well and draw up a few buckets of water." Reply, "Let someone else do it, **I can't do everything and go to mill too.**"

I do declare

Meaning: A phrase of exclamation.

Phrase in use: Charles says Uncle Shell always said, "**I do declare!**" That's when he wanted to drive home a point.

I have a crow to pick with you, I have a bone to pick with you

Meaning: The Southern version is, **I have a crow to pick with you** while Northerners say **I have a bone to pick with you**. Both mean the same, a grievance or complaint against someone.

Phrase in use: "Hey Mamie! **I've got a crow to pick with you**, old sister!" Now what in the world has Mamie done this time? Maybe someone has traced a bit of that juicy gossip she's been spreading back to her.

I wouldn't be caught dead in that outfit

Meaning: An uncomplimentary statement about someone's attire.

Phrase in use: The young woman was so scantily dressed that one of the church ladies gasped, "**I wouldn't be caught dead in that outfit!**" (I don't want to be dead in any outfit, do you?)

I'd know your old hide in a tan yard

Meaning: I would recognize you anywhere I met up with you no matter how long it's been since I last saw you.

Phrase in use: Despite the years, **I'd know your old hide in a tan yard.**

Commentary: I got into trouble one time at the Cedar Grove reunion when Vesta Staggs, an old friend and former neighbor, arrived from Detroit to attend the reunion. I hadn't seen her in many years and she asked if I knew who she was. My reply was, "**I'd know your old hide in a tan yard.**"

Well, she thought I was insulting her and was rather huffy for the remainder of the visit and told everyone she met what I had said to her. It must have been the "old" part that upset her.

If that don't beat everything

Meaning: Surprise or disgust.

Phrase in use: They said down at the store that coffee has gone up two cents on the pound. Well **if that don't beat everything**!

Commentary: In the old Andy Griffith show Andy was always saying to Barney, "You beat everything! You know it!"

If you do as well as you look, you'll do fine

Meaning: A compliment usually to a young person.

Phrase in use: "You look great in your cap and gown, young man, and **if you do as well as you look, you'll do fine,**" iterated the proud grandparents upon their grandson's graduation from high school.

I'gan'nies

Meaning: Disgust.

Phrase in use: "**I'gan'nies**, I reckon it's about to rain because my arthritis is acting up again." Probably a shortened version of "by grannies."

I'll be dogged

Meaning: Surprise!

Phrase in use: I'll be dogged! That boy shore has growed a lot since the last time I seen him!

Commentary: The above phrase reminded me of this story and you'll see why at the end. I've seen people in my day that I didn't like but I can truly say that at this juncture of my life, I don't hate anyone. Not true with the two characters in this story from my boyhood days with…

…Andy and Butch

These two neighbors could not stand the sight of each other. Each one seethed with hatred when they met. I cannot recall a single time I ever saw them get near one another that they didn't fight.

If they were meeting on the road, they'd literally run toward each other as fast as they could, and when they got together, the fight was on. They sometimes fought for hours. I've seen them fight 'til they were so tired they'd just lay on the ground bleeding and trembling, each holding tightly onto the other, making sure he did not escape. They'd glare at one another, and after a brief rest, they'd go at it again.

Butch was the larger of the two, and with his name you'd think he'd win every fight. But that was not the case. Although Andy was smaller in stature, he was long and lean, and as gritty a guy as you'll ever see. There was no quit in either of them and there was never a clear-cut winner when they fought.

They were enemies from the first day they met and they would always be enemies, and come what may, they would never be friends.

We boys around school would often egg-on fights when a skirmish began. We didn't have to egg-on these two, and when they started fighting we just stood back and watched. We never tried to intervene because there was no stopping them until they were completely worn out and could no longer move.

No one really cared who won, that is except Billy Buck and Paul Martin Garrett. Billy was my cousin on my mother's side and Paul Martin was my cousin on my daddy's side. You see, Butch was a large, copper colored Chow Chow with a black tongue and a curly tail, while Andy was an Airedale with wiry whiskers on his long muzzle, and a coat of gray, stiff hair. Butch belonged to Billy and Andy belonged to Paul Martin. The relationship between the Chow Chow and the Airedale often led to strained relations between the two owners, but never to the extent of the disdain the two dogs held for each other.

I'll bound you

Meaning: Said instead of "I'll bet you."

Phrase in use: Ed reasoned, **"I'll bound you** it frosts tonight if the clouds clear out." Peggy replied, "Oh, no! It'll kill all of my flowers if it does!"

I'll bust your hide

Meaning: A serious threat to unruly kids.

Phrase in use: When Mother said **I'll bust your hide**, we straightened up right quick.

Commentary: The mothers were the disciplinarians back then. Dads were the enforcers, or at least that's how it was at our house.

I'll dance at your wedding

Meaning: A pledge of indebtedness. Spoken when requesting a favor or when someone had done them a good turn.

Phrase in use: If you'll put in a good word for me with Patty, **I'll dance at your wedding**. Then, if I get a date with her, **I'll dance at your wedding with cow bells on.**

I'll do in a pinch

Meaning: Just about the same or could be better, could be worse.

Phrase in use: Ask Carolyn how she is and the answer is always, "**I'll do in a pinch.**" And then she may add, "**I'm better'n snuff and not half as messy.**"

I'll give you to know

Meaning: Just so it's clearly understood.

Phrase in use: Lucy bragged, "I made the honor roll and **I'll give you to know** that I earned it!"

Commentary: Even if you earned it there are those who still think you cheated.

I'll knock you so high the birds will build a nest in your pockets before you hit the ground

Meaning: A threat attributed to a cousin, Joe Garrett.

Phrase in use: "You cuss me again and **I'll knock you so high the birds will build a nest in your pockets before you hit the ground.**" Reply, "Yeah, you and whose army?"

I'll knock you to kingdom come

Meaning: A threat that meant you were about to be hit really hard, but never was anyone knocked all the way to kingdom come, or maybe they were just ashamed to tell it.

Phrase in use: The boys would say, **"I'll knock you to kingdom come."** while the girls would usually threaten, **"I'll slap you to kingdom come**." Ouch! That hurts just thinking about getting slapped that hard!

I'll law ye

Meaning: They would take you to court or sue in a court of law.

Phrase in use: "If you don't pay off that note I signed for you, **I'll law ye,** in a court of law," Mr. Bimbo threatened.

Commentary: This writer is reminded of an incident that a friend used to tell. He was walking through the woods to visit a neighbor when he heard someone coming up the path and it sounded as though they were arguing, so he stepped behind a large tree to see what was going on.

It turned out to be John and his wife, Dee, who lived just down the path he was walking. John was in front and Dee was close behind with a long hick'ry withe. Every few steps, she'd swing the switch around John's britches' legs and he would jump about two feet off the ground and say, "You better not hit me again, if you do **I'll law ye.**" He would repeat the statement over and over each time she would swing the switch, whether or not she hit him.

No one ever learned what the argument was about but it was clearly understood who the dominant person in that relationship was.

I'll tan your leather, I'll skin your hide, I'll bust your britches

Meaning: A whuppin'. Example: **"I'll skin your hide,** little girl, if'n you don't straighten yourself up and start acting like a young lady." All three are admonishments and mean the same thing.

Phrase in use: Be quiet, little man, or **I'll tan your leather** and if you keep muttering **I'll bust your britches** for you.

I'll wring your jaws

Meaning: About to be slapped hard on the face.

Phrase in use: "You call me that name again, young man, and **I'll wring your jaws** for you." If it came from a girl it was usually, "**I'll smack your jaws** if you hit me again."

I'm rough and tough and hard to bluff

Meaning: A boastful statement quoted by most of the boys around Cedar Grove School, usually before a fight started.

Phrase in use: A way of bragging after winning a fight. "**I'm rough and tough and hard to bluff** so you'd better learn to leave me alone."

Commentary: Old Butch thought he was the toughest dog in Dogtown but Andy thought the same of himself. What a fight! You could just tell when they snarled and growled at one another each was thinking, "**I'm rough and tough and hard to bluff.**"

If he don't like it, he'll just have to lump it

Meaning: He'll just have to make the best of a bad situation.

Phrase in use: Stump shore is mad about Cal shooting his dog last week, but **if he don't like it he'll just have to lump it.** After all, his dog had just killed Cal's old tom cat that he'd had for years.

Commentary: Origin unknown but it may be from "a lump of leaven" as used in the Bible.

If nothing happens no more than a shoestring breaks

Meaning: To plan to do it if nothing else intervenes that would hinder or delay it.

Phrase in use: "So you plan to meet me in town Saturday to go to the show?" Reply, "**If nothing happens no more than a shoestring breaks**, I'll be there."

Commentary: Going to the show on Saturday was a ritual in most families during the 1930's and 1940's. Tickets cost 10 or 15 cents for adults then.

If the plow stands

Meaning: Used almost exclusively in the Garrett household. It means a person is bound and determined to do a thing no matter what the cost or outcome.

Phrase in use: Dib will go to the County Fair **if the plow stands,** and in his case it usually did stand at least once a year. (Hey, Dib! The fair starts next week. Hope you got your corn laid by.)

Commentary: Last year when he only lacked about 10 rows having his corn crop laid by, Dib took out at dinnertime, went and ate, and walked to town to the fair. His neighbor said those last ten corn rows just grew up with weeds and were never harvested. Dib sure did love to go to the fair.

If wishes were haystacks, there'd be no poor cattle

Meaning: Admonishment for "over wishing."

Phrase in use: Mother said this often especially around Christmas time when we'd looking in the Sears & Roebuck catalogue and wishing for everything in it. For example, "I wish Santa would bring me a real pony." Mother's reply, **"If wishes were haystacks there'd be no poor cattle."** Poor means they were underfed and very skinny or "lean-fleshed" as those described to Joseph in Pharaoh's dream in the book of Genesis, Chapter 41.

If you didn't but know it

Meaning: Bragging or boasting and showing great confidence.

Phrase in use: We're going to the State Fair Saturday **if you didn't but know it!** And we may go Saturday week, too! So just put that in your pipe and smoke it!

If you plan to fry him for a fool, you'd better make sure you have plenty of grease

Meaning: Describing the extent of a person's foolishness, or it might imply that the person could be smarter than he looks or acts; which, in many cases, was the absolute truth.

Phrase in use: That young man is a lot smarter than he looks and **if you plan to fry him for a fool, you'd better make sure you have plenty of grease.**

Commentary: Recording this brings to memory a story about two locals whose names have been changed in this telling. Webster defines an oaf as a stupid or clumsy person. The person in this story may have been oafish in appearance, but was certainly intelligent enough to put a smart, sassy lawyer in his place in this account of…

…The Lawyer and the Oafish Man

Malcolm was a large man, and much older than me as I was approaching adolescence. He was big with coarse features and a deep voice that roared when he talked, and yet he was exceptionally kind and gentle in nature. I was very fond of him and we often swapped comic books, as we both loved reading.

A few weeks after we'd made the swap, I'd walk the distance to his house and we'd visit for a while discussing some of our favorite comic book characters, and then we'd "trade back." We both liked to keep our originals because they were, of course, our favorites. Oh, how I'd like to have back that large stack that I'd accumulated during my childhood, but they all were destroyed by the fire that burned down our family home on New Year's Day in 1955.

Another common interest Malcolm and I shared was a love for the Western movies that were shown at the Ritz Theater on Saturday afternoons. Just as sure as Saturday came, you could find him making the circuit with the crowd around the courthouse square looking in the windows of the stores and shops that lined the business district of our little town.

It happened that the two, Malcolm and the cocky lawyer, were walking in opposite directions on the sidewalk that Saturday, when they met abruptly and both had to stop because of the crowd pressing around them. The lawyer, Z.T. Warsaw, agitated by the large person blocking his path, glared angrily up at the oafish man and, expecting to embarrass him, asked in his high, shrill voice, "Is it cold up there?"

Without blinking or even having to think for a second about his answer, Malcolm replied in his booming voice, "Monkeys can climb. Climb up and see!"

Several people witnessed the incident and, without a doubt, most were happy to see the lawyer "brought down a peg" as we say around here.

In the family way

Meaning: Making reference to a pregnant girl or woman.

Phrase in use: Lora is **in the family way** again.

Commentary: That's what it meant but we children weren't ever allowed to say that. The word "pregnant" was a definite no-no. Herman surmised: "Leck's family is going to get bigger next year." Reply, "Yep, I hear his wife is **in the family way** again and, if I'm counting right, that will make them ten." It's true, there were ten children in their family; seven boys and three girls.

In the short rows

Meaning: Said in reference to the time when a job is almost finished. Oh! How we appreciated those short rows! Thanks again, Finis. If you hadn't laid off those "lands" just exactly right, we'd all still be in the long rows and chopping out corn in the hot, Tennessee sun.

Phrase in use: Referred to the way the corn rows were laid off at the sides of the field. They were always shorter than the ones in the middle. "We'll soon be finished kids, we're **in the short rows** now."

Independent as a hog on ice

Meaning: Coming from the author's mother, it meant being very independent.

Phrase in use: I declare, that child is as **independent as a hog on ice**.

Commentary: Thinking about this phrase it could also mean that the child was very dependent. A hog on ice could not maneuver very well due to the shape of his cloven feet. He would surely need help in getting off a frozen pond or lake.

Ish'taters

Meaning: Referring to Irish potatoes as heard from my Daddy and Aunt Ida. She called them "arsh 'taters"

Phrase in use: Them **ish'taters** sure were good. Pass the platter around again, please.

Is he handy

Meaning: Inquiring whether the person needed is nearby or will it be difficult to reach him.

Phrase in use: "I want to speak to Paul, **is he handy?**" asked Ed. Eula's reply, "Why no, he's out of pocket right now."

It takes all kinds to make a world

Meaning: Quoted when someone you know well, or maybe even a stranger, did something "out of character" or unexpected of him — something you'd not think he would do.

Phrase in use: "I sure never thought he'd marry a city girl." Reply, "Yep, guess the old saying is true, **It takes all kinds to make a world**." Some might say, **"It takes all kinds of people to make a world."**

Commentary: That's why the United States is called *The Melting Pot of the World*.

It'll all come out in the wash

Meaning: Mother often said this, as did other members of the family. It meant that things would be all right in the end and if not the truth would finally be known.

Phrase in use: They accused their neighbor, Sam, of stealing corn; however, Rev. Owen didn't believe a word of it, but stated, "If it is true **it'll all come out in the wash**."

It'll push us

Meaning: Pressed for time.

Phrase in use: "Drive a little faster Millard, **it'll push us** to be home by midnight as it is now." Millard's reply, "I tried to tell you we should have left earlier."

It'll never be noticed on a galloping horse

Meaning: From my sister Maxine, meaning, it's of little significance or it won't be noticed.

Phrase in use: "I can't go! Look at this little spot on my blouse." Reply, "Don't worry about that tiny smudge, **it'll never be noticed on a galloping horse."**

It's as broad as it is long

Meaning: Used by many to illustrate that it was the same either way no matter what the issue.

Phrase in use: Country boy: "We can go down the path or take the road." City boy: "**It's as broad as it is long,** so let's take the road. It's easier walking than the path."

It's better to have it and not need it than to need and not have it

Meaning: It's better to take everything and not use it all than to take a little and need something you don't have.

Phrase in use: Most of the old timers usually said, **"It's better to have it and not need it than to need it and not have it,"** when loading the wagon to go to work.

Commentary: Could be applied to a lady packing for a trip. They always seem to take more than they need yet still don't have everything they want. The husband's unpopular remark, "Why not just drive two vehicles and take everything we can load?" Then adding more unpopularly, "Maybe we should just rent a moving van and take everything we own." (And that's when the fight started.)

J

Jack of all trades

Meaning: Referring to someone who has the unique ability to do almost any job with little effort.

Phrase in use: "I'll bet Uncle Jake can fix it, he's a **jack of all trades**." Reply, "He's a **jack of all trades** but master of none."

Jake-leg preacher

Meaning: Used to describe an amateur or an uneducated person preaching the Gospel.

Phrase in use: He's just another little **Jake-leg preacher** that comes around from time to time and holds revivals, but he can really preach.

Jaylarky

Meaning: Referencing a person they knew little about or perhaps someone acting a bit strange.

Phrase in use: "Who was that **Jaylarky** running off his mouth about the President?" Reply, "I don't know but one thing's for sure, he ain't from around here."

Jig time

Meaning: Describing quick or fast.

Phrase in use: "We can cut that wood in **Jig time.**" Reply, "We'd better be getting started right away because winter's going to be here soon."

Commentary: Jigs are fiddle tunes that are played fast and that could be the origin of this phrase.

Joe Sorrels

Meaning: This saying may be unique to Cousin Joe and his father. They always used it with the word "scared." It meant extremely scared.

Phrase in use: You scared the **Joe Sorrels** out of me! Don't do that again!

Joshing

Meaning: About like **gassing** — it meant joking or teasing.

Phrase in use: Don't get mad. I've just been **joshing** with you all along.

Jubberish

Meaning: Nervous or jumpy.

Phrase in use: That young mule is a little **jubberish** around strangers and he could hurt you if he gets spooked.

Just an old plug

Meaning: Often heard when a trade was taking place. It meant the item in discussion was worth very little.

Phrase in use: "What do you have to trade on today, Houkus?" Reply, "Nothing, **just an old plug** knife that somebody got off on me last week."

Just as leave

Meaning: Making no difference, one might instead say "just as soon."

Phrase in use: "We're out of sweet milk and all we have is sour milk, so what do you want to drink?" Reply, "That's all right, I'd **just as leave** have buttermilk as sweet milk anyway."

Just between you and me and the gatepost

Meaning: I'll tell you but keep the subject matter a secret.

Phrase in use: Just between you and me and the gatepost, I think they're already married and just keeping it a secret till they save up enough money to go to Indiana, but you better not tell that.

Just doing around, Just doing around here

Meaning: Usually the answer given when one was asked, "What are you doing?"

Phrase in use: The reply was often, "Not much, **just doing around here.**" Sometimes adding, "A little bit of everything and not much of nothing."

Just here a few days ago

Meaning: The answer often given if asked when something happened. Attributed to no particular individual, the phrase enjoyed general usage back in their day.

Phrase in use: "When did you say the accident happened?" Reply, "Why, **just here a few days ago**, I think." No one knows why the word "here" was added to the reply.

Commentary: In their "relaxed and laid back Southern culture" it seemed that there were no absolutes. They (we) seemingly shied away from anything definite, especially when answering questions such as the above answer. It's possible that the person answering knew exactly when the accident occurred but did not want to be penned down to an exact date.

K

Katy bar the door

Meaning: Denoting the fact that it's all over.

Phrase in use: It's **Katy bar the door** now 'cause that old fence is so bad we'll never be able to keep those cows in since they got into the hay field and tasted that good clover.

Keel over dead

Meaning: Eminent death.

Phrase in use: "If Sam keeps eating like he does and putting on weight, he's likely to **keel over dead** one of these days, and maybe very soon." Reply, "That's true but look at me, I can't say a word about Sam. That'd be just like the pot calling the kettle black."

Keep house

Meaning: A "housemaid" or domestic help who manages the household.

Phrase in use: My mother came down with pneumonia when I was a baby, and one of the neighbor girls came in to **keep house** for our family during her illness.

Kindly

Meaning: It means "a little bit" or "sort of." Not at all related to the word "kind" but meaning almost, somewhat, or nearly.

Phrase in use: I **kindly** like poke sallet now, don't you?

Know him/her like a book

Meaning: Well acquainted with a person. Knowing all about his personality and behavior.

Phrase in use: "I **know him like a book**, and I'm betting he'll ask me to marry him before Christmas," said Sweet Charlotte of her boyfriend. (But, Sweet Charlotte, supposing he **knows you like a book**, would you still expect a proposal before Christmas?)

L

Lainard

Meaning: Commonly referred to as a lantern.

Phrase in use: Almost everyone owned a **lainard** instead of a flashlight back then.

Larapin

Meaning: Something very good and tasty.

Phrase in use: Them new molasses is **larapin;** no they're **larapin** good.

Lay off a land

Meaning: Term used to describe the first round when plowing a field for planting.

Phrase in use: "Finis, **lay off a land** so we'll have a few short rows." Reply, "You know I always do, James."

Commentary: My cousin, Finis Buck, would always **lay off a land** in a way to have short rows even if the field was square. He knew how those short rows would be appreciated when it was time to chop out the corn and pull the fodder.

Lazed

Meaning: A verb meaning doing nothing at all except being lazy all the day long.

Phrase in use: "Ma, did them kids get the garden weeded out like I told them before I left?" Reply, "Why no Pap, they've **lazed** around here all morning waiting for it to rain and it never did. I told them a dozen times to get to work but they ain't pulled a weed."

Commentary: Seldom heard today but one time enjoyed frequent usage. The word was a form of lazy and not to be confused with the past tense of the verb "lase" which is "lased" a new word brought about by the invention of the laser light. The word "laser" is an acronym for Light Amplification by Simulated Emission of Radiation the past tense of which is "lased."

Lazy as all get out

Meaning: About as lazy as one could become.

Phrase in use: "They say Sally's kids are all just a lazy bunch and are too lazy to brush off the flies." Reply, "I guess they're just as lazy as all get out." Still others would say that they're lazier than kyarn.

Lazy as kyarn

Meaning: Their word for "carrion." The phrase was used when referring to an extremely lazy person. "Kyarn" also meant something stinking badly.

Phrase in use: Abe was a hard worker but he raised a bunch of boys that are as **lazy as kyarn.**

Least said — soon'st mended

Meaning: The less said about an unpleasant matter or something bad, the quicker it will go away or get better.

Phrase in use: "Shore was bad about them two falling out over a dog but, you know what they say, **least said-soon'st mended.** So let's not talk about it anymore until the issue is settled," stated a close friend and relative. Reply from a neighbor, "Really, there's no more to be said until those two long-time friends come to their senses, and stop acting like children, and make up."

Leb'em

Meaning: The number eleven.

Phrase in use: The number eleven has three syllables, but **leb'em** has only two; proving again that **they said it their way.** To pronounce it their way you may rhyme it with **seb'em** meaning the number "seven."

Let's motor

Meaning: Let's get moving and often said after stopping for a break while travelling.

Phrase in use: Buford was feeling better when he said, "We've had lunch and gassed up the car so **let's motor.**"

Commentary: This is a newer saying attributed to Buford Nivens.

Liable

Meaning: Nothing to do with the law but likely, or apt to do something.

Phrase in use: It's **liable** to patch up a cloud and rain if the wind keeps blowing from the West.

Life gets teedjus

Meaning: Sometimes our daily lives are tiring, even boring, meaning "tedious."

Phrase in use: I get tired of doing these chores day after day. Yes, **life gets teedjus,** don't it!

Like a chicken with its head cut off

Meaning: Disorganized approach to a task. Unfocused and scatterbrained.

Phrase in use: Look how he's going about fixing that car. It'll never run again with him working **like a chicken with its head cut off.**

Commentary: To understand this clearly, you need to have seen **a chicken with its head cut off.**

Like a wiggle worm in hot ashes

Meaning: Being very nervous and jittery.

Phrase in use: Gabe's **like a wiggle worm in hot ashes** when he dances.

Commentary: "William had to sit on the front row at church last Sunday night and the poor boy was **like a wiggle worm in hot ashes.**" Reply, "I've never seen a boy so nervous in all my born days but no wonder, did you see that stern look on her dad's face?" (It was said that William only had two dates with her and that was both: The first and the last.)

Like something the cats drug in

Meaning: Description of someone who looks terrible. That person could have been in a fight or stayed out all night carousing.

Phrase in use: "Heavens Chick! What happened to you? You look **like something the cats drug in!**" Chick's response, "I know it, and I feel like it too."

Like the pot calling the kettle black

Meaning: An accuser being just as bad or guilty as the one he is accusing, except he can't see his own blackness.

Phrase in use: "Jake said that John was the biggest liar he has ever seen." Reply, "That's just **like the pot calling the kettle black,** because Jake himself is known to be the biggest liar around."

Commentary: In frontier days, much of the cooking was done by hanging a pot over the fire in the fireplace. This served a dual purpose: One, it saved wood and two, it avoided heating the kitchen in summertime. A large black kettle was used outside for rendering lard, making lye soap, and washing the clothes. Setting or hanging directly over the fire for a long period of time resulted in both pots becoming very black thus the saying, "That's **like the pot calling the kettle black."** One was just as black as the other.

Lives by the clock

Meaning: Someone who is always aware of the   time and on schedule.

Phrase in use: My sister is never late, because she literally **lives by the clock.**

Loaded for bear

Meaning: Someone who is totally equipped to handle any need or crisis that may arise.

Phrase in use: Men, we've a big job ahead of us but we're equipped to handle it. So, bring it on, we're **loaded for bear!**

Loblolly

Meaning: The act of children finding a place where silt had been deposited after a rain. They would stomp on this spot until it became mushy and squiggled between their toes, and up to the ankles or even the knees sometimes.

Phrase in use: "Kids! Get out of that **loblolly**, get in here and wash up, and don't track mud all over the house! It's supper time," yelled Ma.

Lock, stock, and barrel

Meaning: Disgusted with a lack of success. Giving up and tossing the lot.

Phrase in use: If things don't change around here, I'm going to sell out **lock, stock, and barrel** and leave this place.

Lollygag

Meaning: To be slow and wasting time.

Phrase in use: Don't **lollygag** around! Try to be on time just once!

Love them to death

Meaning: To be truly fond of someone.

Phrase in use: "You say you've met the new neighbors too?" Reply, "Yes, we have! And don't you just **love them to death?"**

Commentary: I don't recall where I heard it or who said it but this little verse seems to belong here: *To love the world is no great chore, but it's difficult to love the neighbor next door.* How true! It can be difficult to love even those who are family if they are contrary.

Lying like a dog a'trottin'

Meaning: Referring to a lie or many lies.

Phrase in use: "You can just look at him and tell he's **lying like a dog** a'trottin.'" Reply, "They say if his lips are moving he's lying."

Commentary: The writer is reminded of his childhood when he owned dogs. They always trotted along in front of the farm wagon any time there was a job or a trip. Upon coming to a fork in the road the dogs always amazed them by taking the correct turn as if they had read their minds or over-heard them talking and understood each word.

M

Madder'n an old wet hen
Madder'n an old wet settin' hen

Meaning: Showing extreme anger.

Phrase in use: When Pete gets mad, he's sometimes **madder'n an old wet hen**.

Commentary: I'm reminded of the time I saw Daddy get **madder'n an old wet settin' hen,** only this time he was mad at an old rooster. We had a large Rhode Island Red rooster that ruled the chicken yard at that time. He had long spurs and a sharp beak, and made life miserable for anyone who might amble into his territory. He strutted around like the King of Siam and flogged anyone who came near him.

My cousin, Shelvie (Buck) Dubree, was very young at this time, maybe four or five years old, and was at our house often after her mother died. One day, she was playing in the yard near our old well shed when the rooster thought she had transgressed his domain. He jumped on little Shelvie and began spurring her unmercifully.

It happened that day that Daddy was nearby and, picking up a stick of stove wood, he taught that old rooster a lesson he wouldn't remember very long. You see, come suppertime that evening Old Rhodie's fat carcass resided on a bed of dumplings in the largest kettle my mother had.

After supper, the only reminder of that old Rhode Island Red rooster was the pleasant aroma of chicken and dumplings that lingered throughout the house, and the spur marks on little Shelvie's back.

Make water

Meaning: Adults taught their children to say this when they needed to use the restroom.

Phrase in use: Please don't leave until I get back. I'm about to go **make water**.

Making light

Meaning: Making fun of or teasing unmercifully. Having nothing to do with electricity or a light switch.

Phrase in use: "Mama, them big boys is **making light** of my shirt. They claim it was made out of a feed sack and I thought it was store-bought." Mama's reply, "Well child, it is made out of a feed sack, but don't you be ashamed to stand right up and tell them it is. Just tell them you're proud to have a mother who can sew."

May'a did

Meaning: A saying unique to my friend Guyland meaning: May have done so.

Phrase in use: "Do you think they finished their spring plowing before the big rain yesterday?" asked Gerald. **"May'a did,"** answered Guyland, "they had plenty of help from the neighbors."

Mealy-mouth

Meaning: Beating around the bush and not saying what you really think. Not really wanting to face the issue.

Phrase in use: Well, don't **mealy-mouth** around about it, just come out and say what you think.

More ways than one to skin a cat

Meaning: There are many ways to accomplish something when you think about how to approach it in a different manner.

Phrase in use: They found that using a crowbar instead of a pulley worked just as well and was much more efficient, proving once again that there are **more ways than one to skin a cat.**

Commentary: But the big question is: "Why would anyone want to skin a cat? It's common knowledge that no one wears "kitten britches" nowadays."

Mosey on down

Meaning: Moving slowly or not under any pressure to get there.

Phrase in use: "We'd better **mosey on down** to the creek bank if we're planning on having fish for supper." Reply, "Let's go, 'cause I'm already getting hungry."

Motorcating

Meaning: Meaning about the same as cruising.

Phrase in use: Gary just went **motorcating** down the road in that old car he bought but, he wasn't going more than 20 miles per hour.

Mountain out of a mole hill

Meaning: Don't make things worse than they really are.

Phrase in use: "Children, this is not a big problem so let's not make a **mountain out of a mole hill** by gossiping about it," stated Papa.

Much obliged

Meaning: Older expression meaning "thank you."

Phrase in use: Much obliged, neighbor, for helping me with the spring plowing.

N

Naked as a picked bird

Meaning: Degree of nudeness.

Phrase in use: They come upon the boys skinny-dipping and each was **naked as a picked bird,** but they jumped right out on the bank anyway trying to get to their clothes.

Commentary: Observing some of today's bikinis, skinny-dipping may have made a comeback.

Never amount to a hill of beans

Meaning: Little was expected of the person in question — maybe just a "n'er-do-well."

Phrase in use: "He'll **never amount to a hill of beans.**" Reply, "Nah, he's almost too lazy to feed hisself, and he's kindly short on brainpower."

Never has been but one and he's both of them

Meaning: Said about someone deemed odd, eccentric, or "quare."

Phrase in use: Never has been but one and he's both of them, remarked Tom, speaking of his neighbor.

Commentary: This expression is attributed to "Tapper" Tom, an individual who lived up the road from us and who was literally my daddy's right hand man. He was always at our place doing some kind of work. He had little formal education but was very intelligent and talented. He was skilled in doing about any job that needed to be done on a farm or in the log woods. Oh yes, he was the "nicknamer" for the entire community.

Not long for this world

Meaning: Time on earth is short and his days are numbered.

Phrase in use: "Poor old Bob, he's a very sick mule, and considering his age and all, and I'm afraid he's **not long for this world.**" The Veterinarian agreed, "I wouldn't spend any more money on him if I were in your place." That was a tough decision because their children loved old Bob like one of the family.

A little bit of everything and not much of nothing

Meaning: Not very busy.

Phrase in use: Often the answer to the question, "What are you doing?" was, **"A little bit of everything and not much of nothing."**

Nuss

Meaning: To hold a baby on the knees, not to actually let him nurse.

Phrase in use: Probably came from the Negro dialect meaning "nurse." "Let me **nuss** the baby for a while, he'll be more content on my lap than he will being passed from one to another as you're doing."

O

One t'other" "One t'other'n'

Meaning: The first expression meaning one or the other, the second meaning one or the other one.

Phrase in use: "Them twin boys, I can't tell one from **t'other**." Reply, "I can, one has a tiny mole under his chin and **t'other'n** don't."

Once a man, twice a child

Meaning: That period of life known as a "second childhood."

Phrase in use: "Ezra just had his 90th birthday and he acts as though he's entering his second childhood." Juliet's reply, "I've always heard it said, **once a man, twice a child,** so I guess he is.**"

Operating on a shoestring

Meaning: Barely getting by financially and just hanging on.

Phrase in use: "I wish we could buy your place but we're just **operating on a shoestring** right now." Reply, "Well, I wish I could sell it to you but I understand that you're about to go broke."

Out of pocket

Meaning: A person or thing is not where it should be.

Phrase in use: Billups is always **out of pocket** when there's work to be done, but he manages to turn early up on payday.

Out of sorts

Meaning: Not in a pleasant mood.

Phrase in use: "What's got you kids all **out of sorts** this morning?" The kids reply, "You should know! You got us up too early!"

Out'n the light

Meaning: Heard in Pennsylvania, it means turn out the lights.

Phrase in use: "Don't forget to **out'n the light** when you go to bed," cautioned Gail, "electricity is high these days, and we're not rich you know."

Overall britches

Meaning: What we now call Levis or blue jeans.

Phrase in use: "Crock had on a brand new pair of **overall britches** with a new white shirt and necktie at the funeral last week," said Teddy. Reply, "Yeah, he did look kindly dressed up."

Over the hill

Meaning: Getting old. Better days are past and gone.

Phrase in use: All my friends are getting on **over the hill** now and I'm right behind and climbing fast.

Commentary: Yes, the saying is true, it is lonely at the top.

P

Paper poke

Meaning: A brown paper bag. What they used instead of plastic grocery bags.

Phrase in use: "I'll put your dinner in a **paper poke** so it will be easy for you to carry," said Jessie as she packed the school lunches.

Past going

Meaning: Term alluding to potential death.

Phrase in use: "I saw Uncle Cal today and the poor thing is just about **past going**." Reply, "I know! That old rheumatiz' has just about got him down, and I do declare, it'll be the death of him yet."

Patch up a cloud and rain

Meaning: Attributed to this writer's daddy. This phrase was often used in situations where it looked like it was about to rain.

Phrase in use: "Rest fast boys, it may **patch up a cloud and rain** before we can make in home," said B.B. anticipating a rain.

Peachtree tea, Hick'rey tea Sassafras tea

Meaning: A "whuppin'" with a switch usually administered by mamas. Daddies used their belt or a leather strop when they needed to discipline while, most of the time, teachers used a paddle.

Phrase in use: "Bring me a limb off that peach tree, little Missy. I'm going to give you a dose of **peachtree tea,** and if that don't settle you down, we'll try **hick'rey** and **sassafras tea** too, and I don't mean the kind you sip on. We're trying to make a lady of you."

Penitentiary 'fence'

Meaning: Shortened version of "penitentiary offence." This was a continual threat used to make their children mind.

Phrase in use: You'd better not shoot those glass brackets off the telephone poles. You know, it's a **penitentiary 'fence** to do that.

Commentary: They made great sport of shooting those glass brackets that held the telephone wires to the poles. If a .22 rifle wasn't available, they would use a sling shot or break them by throwing rocks.

Peppering down

Meaning: Describing the degree of rain, snow, or sleet.

Phrase in use: Gracie said, "It's **peppering down** rain, can't you hear it hitting the tin roof?" Martin questioned, "Are you sure? That sounds like sleet to me."

Perish the thought

Meaning: According to my sister Maxine, she heard this phrase being used by our Pa Garrett meaning, "don't even think about it."

Phrase in use: "Pa, do you think we're on the brink of war again?" Reply, "Mercy no child! **Perish the thought!**"

Persnickety

Meaning: Being very particular or maybe just a little conceited.

Phrase in use: "That new girl always acts a little **persnickety** around me." Reply, "Well I think she's just downright stuck up."

Pickyunish

Meaning: Being very particular about most everything, especially food.

Phrase in use: "Little Eddie sure looks thin. I'll bet he don't weigh 80 pounds soaking wet." Reply, "Well, no wonder, it's 'cause he so **pickyunish** about his eating. He'll need rocks in his pockets to hold him down when the March winds blow."

Piddle

Meaning: To go slow or waste time.

Phrase in use: You kids, don't **piddle** around playing with that dog 'till you're late for school.

Commentary: Miss Stella says you have been late every day this week and she won't tolerate your tardiness any longer. She says next time it's the paddle. (Ouch! That hurts!)

Pistol

Meaning: Same as "tooter" and may refer to an adult or a child, or maybe a rowdy teen-ager.

Phrase in use: They say you'd better watch out for that young man, because he's a **pistol.**

Pitch a fit, Throw a fit

Meaning: To get very angry about something.

Phrase in use: "Rasco's going to **pitch a fit** when he finds out about his boy wrecking their new car." Reply, "We'd be surprised if he don't **throw a fit** this time."

Pit'cher

Meaning: Word used instead of "picture."

Phrase in use: "Do you have a **pit'cher** of the new baby?" asked Audrey. Proud Papa's reply, "Do I have a **pit'cher**? Here's an album full of them taken just right after Jr. was born!"

Commentary: The great, singer/songwriter Hank Williams pronounced it this way in his recording of *"Pictures from Life's Other Side."* It's been said that a word that is mispronounced or used in error can often lead to a hit record as it did in this recording.

Plague take it

Meaning: Used instead of darn, dang, or heck.

Phrase in use: Plague take it, it'll take us 'til midnight if we have to walk all the way home.

Commentary: Often they did walk all the way home from town after "staying over" for the late show. The distance varied from 8 to 10 miles.

P'laver

Meaning: Variation of the word "palaver" meaning you talk and argue way too much.

Phrase in use: "Now boys, don't **p'laver** around all morning about doing this work. You all know it must be finished before we take out for dinner," said the Foreman of the crew.

Commentary: Most children will **p'laver** on and on if they think it will delay the work that's been assigned them to do. It works too. There were two brothers that would intentionally do it wrong knowing their dad would do it himself.

Plum tuckered out

Meaning: Very tired.

Phrase in use: "You girls quit wagging that baby around. Can't you see, he's **plum tuckered out** from being handled so much?" said Ivory.

Podunk Holler

Meaning: A name used if one wanted to associate anyone coming from a nowhere place.

Phrase in use: If a person were overtly shy or a little naïve they might be asked if they were from **Podunk Holler.**

Poke sallet

Meaning: A plant that grows wild over most of the United States and many other countries.

Phrase in use: C'mon over for supper, mama's cooking a mess of **poke sallet.**

Commentary: This plant is abundant here in May when it may be gathered in the wild. It is boiled then fried in bacon grease with eggs, and scrambled in a black skillet. It is good when eaten with hoe cakes or cornbread. When mature, the plant bears a purple berry that will stain the clothing of young boys who play in the "poke berry patch."

Mamas don't like it one little bit, the stains that is, and it seems that the men folks like **poke sallet** better that the women folks do. It's been said that the Native Americans used the berries to color their clothes and make war paint for their faces.

'Pon my honor

Meaning: Exclamation expressing surprise. The phrase actually went "**Upon my honor**" but most left off the "U".

Phrase in use: "'**Pon my honor**! I never knew that!" Peggy June has shortened it even more. She just says, "Well 'pon..." and stops there.

Pone of bread

Meaning: It could be a pone of loaf bread, or a pone of cornbread but never "a loaf of bread" when they said it.

Phrase in use: "I'm hungry, what's to eat?" growled Turley. Reply, "There's a **pone of cornbread** in the warming closet, but you'll have to go to the spring to get the buttermilk."

Poor as church mice

Meaning: The condition of being very poor.

Phrase in use: Them people over across the mountain are as **poor as church mice.**

Poor as Job's turkey

Meaning: An old expression describing a very poor condition and maybe even dating back to Job's day.

Phrase in use: "The family that just moved in from the North is as **poor as Job's turkey.**" Reply, "Yep, they'll need some help before winter is over if none of them can find work."

Poorly

Meaning: Describing a person's health condition and always in a negative way.

Phrase in use: "How are you today, Uncle Jim?" Reply, "Not good a'tall, I've been feeling **poorly** for several days now."

Prize

Meaning: Not a gift nor a reward but rather a verb meaning to "pry."

Phrase in use: Get a crowbar and see if you can **prize** up the edge of the wagon bed and we'll try to get the wheel back on.

Pshaw or Pshaw, by-jacks

Meaning: Meaning about the same as "Aw heck," and sometimes adding, **by-jacks** for emphasis.

Phrase in use: "**Pshaw**, I don't believe a word that man says." Reply, "Well! **Pshaw! By-Jacks**, it's too late now, he's already been elected to Congress."

Pug ugly

Meaning: Description of a person's appearance.

Phrase in use: Sister Hanks was surely ugly. It was often remarked that she was **pug ugly.**

Commentary: Pug probably referred to a prizefighter or maybe a bulldog. There was a lady in our neighborhood who was **pug ugly**, and sure enough, she had a face that looked like a bulldog. However, she was a very kind and sweet lady and her "turn" certainly didn't match her looks.

Pulled a drunk

Meaning: Meaning about the same as "he got drunk" but not on a binge.

Phrase in use: They say D.T. **pulled a drunk** when his daughter eloped with that smart-aleck boy she'd been dating for only two weeks. But you've got to remember, D.T.'s always looking for an excuse to **pull a drunk.**

Pump knot

Meaning: A swollen place on the head caused by being hit with a stick, a rock, or some other blunt object. Others call it a goose-egg.

Phrase in use: Billy still has a big **pump knot** on his head from being hit with a snowball last week.

Commentary: Cousin Joe would often put a rock in the center of the snowball. That's why it made such a big **pump knot.**

Put the big pot in the little one

Meaning: Describing someone trying to make a big show or impress others.

Phrase in use: "I hear tell the Johnsons threw a big shindig last week when their folks from Ohio come to visit." Reply, "Yeah they really **put the big pot in the little one.**"

Put your money where your mouth is

Meaning: Back up what you are saying with proof.

Phrase in use: What better way to demonstrate its use than through this commentary when Flem demanded of Joe Cephas, **"Put your money where your mouth is."**

Commentary: Cousin Joe Cephas just happened to have a dollar bill in the pocket of his patched-up overall britches that foggy fall morning at Flem's General Store when the argument began. A 100 lb. sack of salt was displayed in the middle of the store and somehow, the discussion centered on the weight of the salt.

Flem argued that the weight was greater because of the dampness in the air and Joe challenged him with the statement that he could carry that bag of salt one mile without stopping to rest no matter how much it weighed. "Put your money where your mouth is," barked Flem, while Joe pulled out the bill and said he'd wager it against all he could eat from the store, and the bet was on.

Now Cousin Joe was a big, strong fourteen-year-old boy, whose craving for food was never satiated. He could eat more than any two or three grown men at one setting and still leave the table hungry, but Joe's eating habits were unbeknownst to the storekeeper.

The small crowd of men and young boys watched and listened intently as a few ground rules were laid out for the contest. It was decided that the oldest man present would hold the dollar bill and to the last house down the road and back would be the distance the sack of salt would have to be carried.

Of course, the men in the group were pulling for Flem and the boys for Joe Cephas, even one or two that he had given a sound thrashing in past days.

Two of the bigger boys dragged the salt to the edge of the store porch as Joe went down the steps to the ground. The load was then eased onto the shoulders of the gangly boy and the contest was underway. In reality, no one expected to see Joe eat his fill of groceries, especially since it was beginning a slow drizzle.

Flem had a grin on his face that seemed to be permanently affixed. He sure liked the feel of those dollar bills even the crinkled and tattered one that had been wagered.

Walking at a steady but moderate pace some of the group said he speeded up just a tiny bit as he made the circle in front of the target house and headed back toward the store. As he approached the anxious group in the yard, it appeared that he could have gone another mile. Then as he neared the porch he walked directly in front of Flem, smiled at him and winked, then turned and backtracked his route about 50 yards before coming back, still carrying his load without stopping or resting.

Joe then dumped the sack of salt on the edge of the porch, bounded up the steps, and dragged it across the floor to its previous station, all the time pointing to things on the shelves that he wanted to eat. Old Flem was reluctant in dishing out the goodies but knew that he could not back down. All the while, the youngster was choosing the most expensive foods he could to rub it in on the older group for doubting his strength.

Flem's face was very long by the time Joe had eaten more than $3 worth of delicacies, and he knew the bill would double in just a few minutes. "How much would you take to just call off the bet and stop right now?" he asked.

Without hesitation, Cousin Joe said, "A $1.50 would do it."

Flem replied that he could bear to give no more than $1.20, and the deal was quickly accepted. After all, Joe came out with his original buck, plus another one-dollar bill and twenty cents in change, not to mention that his stomach was almost filled.

Word soon spread throughout the community about Joe Cephas' strength and no one ever dared bet against him again.

Puttin' on

Meaning: Pretending.

Phrase in use: "That child ain't sick. He's **just puttin'** on to stay out of school," said Patsy of her little brother, Tony.

Commentary: The term **puttin' on** may be old but the practice is still widely used by many young students, especially those who don't like school or perhaps just don't like getting up early to get ready. Nowadays, some children are bullied at school and that is why they feign sickness.

Quare

Meaning: Odd or strange. It meant the same as the word "queer."

Phrase in use: Everyone around here says that Uncle Bud acts **quare.**

Commentary: This story entitled A Little Bit Quare was passed down by the writer's mother, Ove (Buck) Garrett and he never heard it from anyone else. Yes, this story proves that Uncle Bud was...

...A Little Bit Quare

On one occasion at the Martin Garrett place there was a job that required the men to get up early and leave without breakfast. No one remembers the task that was to be completed so early but the workers arose long before daylight and went off to attend it without eating breakfast.

It happened that Ove's half-aunt, Mary (Burgess) Sullivan, and her husband, Uncle Bud, were visiting the Garretts, so Uncle Bud joined the work force for that day and went along to the job site with the others. It was mid-morning before the job was finished and the workers returned to the house, starving from lack of having had breakfast.

Of course, the ladies of the household had been busy all morning preparing for the large number that would be eating the mid-morning meal. Breakfast was ready, so the hungry men could sit right down and eat without further delay.

As Uncle Bud approached the table, he remarked to Ove that he had a splitting headache. "Well, sit right down, Uncle Bud, and I'll bring you a cup of black coffee. That's the reason your head is hurting, you haven't had your morning cup of coffee."

Now it had been said by some that Uncle Bud was **a little bit quare.** Today he would probably be called "eccentric." Uncle Bud's reaction to her diagnosis of the cause of his headache reinforced the belief of most folks that, indeed, he was a little bit quare.

He replied, "Very well, if that's what coffee does to me, don't bring me any. I'll just quit drinking the stuff."

Ove stated later that to the best of her knowledge he never drank another cup of coffee.

Quiateus

Meaning: Unsure of the spelling but this word may be derived from the word "hiatus" since the meaning is somewhat the same. It means put to a stop or halt.

Phrase in use: "Cozby sure put the **quiateus** on that romance between his young daughter and the travelling salesman when he greeted him at the front door with a shotgun on his last visit." Reply, "Yep, they said that the slick-tongued salesman crossed the ridge sailing out dock and hasn't passed this way since."

Quile

Meaning: Coil.

Phrase in use: The boy from the city said, "A snake can't bite you unless he has time to **quile** up, so when you see a snake **quile**, he's about to strike." Country boy's reply, "No, that's not so, that's a myth, because they don't have to **quile** up to strike."

Commentary: The above mention of snakes reminds me of stories I have heard since boyhood about the Hoop Snake, which I soon dismissed as a myth. However, my mother-in-law, Vallie Robbins, declared until her death that she saw one when she was a young girl.

Thinking it was just a local legend that existed only in the South, I was shocked to learn that such stories exist worldwide. According to lore, the snake, when frightened, takes its tail into its mouth, forms a hoop, and rolls down the hill. Its venom is in the tail and if it stings you, you'll surely die within minutes.

One story was that a green tree was in the path of a rolling snake and was struck by the tail. Its leaves withered and the tree died within minutes. Truth or fiction, I cannot say. You be the judge.

"Have you ever heard of the hoop snake?"

_____

_____

_____

R

Rare

Meaning: Not referring to cooking or how you like your steak, this word referred to child discipline by stern counseling or scolding.

Phrase in use: "Mother and Daddy will **rare** on us if we're late getting our work done. Daddy would add words to the phrase sometimes saying, "Get to work and I don't want any **raring** and jareing, or **raring** and scotching about it." But still, we did some griping and complaining.

Rench

Meaning: Having to do with water but nothing related to a wrench, although pronounced the same way.

Phrase in use: I'll wash the dishes if you will **rench** them.

Commentary: The author states that he never knew that **rench** wasn't a word until he learned to read and saw the word "rinse" in print.

Rest fast

Meaning: Phrase is attributed exclusively to the author's daddy since he never heard anyone else use the expression. He would say this only when he had teenage boys working for him; never if there were adult workers present.

Phrase in use: Rest fast boys, we have to get this hay in the dry before it rains.

Riding the big horse

Meaning: Comment from someone who might be a little envious of another's success or popularity.

Phrase in use: "Big Buck's really throwing his money around since he came into his inheritance." Reply, "Yeah, he's **riding the big horse** now but he'll be broke flat before the year is out if he continues to spend his money like he's blowing it now."

Right on the barrel head, howdy

Meaning: You got it exactly right or you nailed it.

Phrase in use: "You like the doghouse I just finished building?" asked young Jim proudly? Marty's reply, "Yes sir, it's **right on the barrel head, howdy!**" Jim figured that meant "perfect" as his head swelled out of his cap and two buttons popped off his shirt as his chest swelled out.

Ring tail twister

Meaning: The same connotation as that applying to "Ringtum" or "Tooter." A derogatory remark referencing a young woman or a child who's out of control.

Phrase in use: "That young lady is going to be a **ring tail twister** if her parents don't get her under control." Reply, "I agree, they say she is already creating a real problem at school, and one more incident will put her in in-school suspension if they don't kick her out of school permanently."

Roached up

Meaning: Neatly combed hair, which is standing up high in front much like the men are wearing their hair today.

Phrase in use: "Shirley had his new shirt on and his hair all **roached up** in front when he attended the picnic last week." Reply, "I noticed that. I think he's got his eye on some girl."

Root hog or die poor

Meaning: Advice to someone having a hard time because they had wasted a good opportunity.

Phrase in use: Well, he had a good job in Ohio and just up and quit it, now he'll just have to **root hog or die poor**, and he needn't expect any help from his neighbors this time.

Roughness

Meaning: High fiber livestock feed.

Phrase in use: You need to always feed some **roughness** with the grain when the mules are being worked hard.

Commentary: At one time this was a commonly used word and probably came from the word "roughage" that was fed to the livestock. It consisted of low protein foods such as hay, fodder, and tops. The latter two, fodder and tops came from the corn plant, the leaves being fodder and the tassels and about 24 inches of stalk being the tops.

Sometimes, the entire corn stalk was cut, ears and all, and stacked into large "shocks" for mule and cow feed. A side benefit was the ambiance they created around Halloween, especially when the pumpkins were ripe and lay scattered around them.

Farmers often kept their children out of school in late summer to pull fodder, tie tops, and cut corn. This created turmoil with the children, deciding which was worse, school work or farm work.

Run into her/him

Meaning: An encounter with someone.

Phrase in use: "Seen Aunt Josie lately?" Reply, "Why I **run into her** and her man, just here the other day."

Runs like a scalded dog

Meaning: Capable of running very fast.

Phrase in use: It's a good running little old car. She's old and don't look too good, but she still **runs like a scalded dog.** I wouldn't be afraid to start to Detroit in her tomorrow!

Run through the flint mill

Meaning: Very tired from having had a bad day.

Phrase in use: Joe Dan looked like he'd been **run through the flint mill** after the Doc gave him that extended stress test.

Commentary: This was a favorite of Cousin Ruby Ray. While visiting her in her declining years and asking how she was feeling she would always reply, "Child, I feel like I've been **run through the flint mill**."

The author has no idea what a flint mill is, or how it works, but there are several locations where the rocks litter the grounds around his property. Many Indian relics, made from flint, have been found in those areas.

This crude drawing depicts what a flint mill would have looked like in Ruby's day or even prior to that era. A person having been run through that would certainly have had a haggard appearance, but think how valuable such a machine would have been

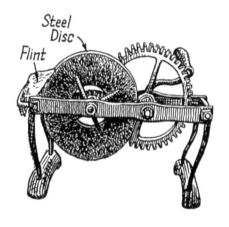

to Native Americans. They had to chisel each arrowhead by hand which was, no doubt, a long and tedious process.

Edwin Garrett

S

Saave

Meaning: An ointment rubbed on the skin commonly called "salve."

Phrase in use: Rubbing some **saave** on a sore can be soothing.

Sailing out dock

Meaning: Leaving in a hurry.

Phrase in use: They were **sailing out dock** when their car hit a tree. This could have come from the term, sailing out of the dock by boat. In their vocabulary it meant travelling extremely fast.

Sallet

Meaning: Cooked greens such as mustard, turnip, spinach, poke sallet or something well-liked or enjoyed.

Phrase in use: "Have you had a mess of poke **sallet** this spring?" or "He's going fishing today and that is just his **sallet.**"

Scarce as hen's teeth

Meaning: Extremely rare.

Phrase in use: Some, including my daddy, pronounced scarce "scace" omitting the "r." "Chestnuts are as **scarce as hen's teeth** hereabouts since the fungal blight killed all our good chestnut trees years ago," he would often say.

School housing

Meaning: A term attributed to a cousin meaning backwards, naïve, or unlearned.

Phrase in use: "Them boys from down the river act like they ain't had no **school housing**." Reply, "Yeah, they'll believe anything you tell them."

Scratch his mad place and get glad

Meaning: Essentially the same as "live with it" or "just suck it up."

Phrase in use: "Pearly was really mad when you pushed her brother into the pond and ruined his new shoes." Reply, "Well, she'll just have to **scratch her mad place and get glad** because the little pest had it coming to him for shooting me in the back with his popgun."

Scrootch

Meaning: To cuddle or get up real close to another person. Rhyme with "pooch."

Phrase in use: **Scrootch** up close to me, I'm freezing to death.

Scrouged

Meaning: A lot of people gathered in a small place. Rhyme with "gouged" to pronounce correctly.

Phrase in use: "My cousins just about **scrouged** me out of bed last night." Reply, "I know! It's difficult sleeping with five in one bed."

Commentary: When company came the young'un's all had to sleep in one bed, two or three at the head and two or three at the foot. It sounds terrible but it was usually fun.

See you in the funny papers

Meaning: A smart-aleck way to say so long when parting, meaning you're so crazy you might appear in the comics.

Phrase in use: "So long, **see you in the funny papers.**" "Maybe, if you don't come out first," was the usual reply.

Set his cap for

Meaning: Stating that he had his mind on a certain girl and was determined to be her boyfriend.

Phrase in use: Little Jackie sure is crazy about Tessie. He **set his cap for** her the first time he laid eyes on her.

Set it down

Meaning: Heard often in the country stores, which were abundant during the WWI and WWII eras meaning "charge it."

Phrase in use: Asked the storekeeper, "How do you want to settle this bill?" Reply, "Just **set it down** and I'll pay you when I sell my chickens in a few days."

Set you up all night before we'll let you go to bed hungry

Meaning: Friendly reassurance of hospitality.

Phrase in use: This statement was often heard when company was leaving after visiting for a while: "If you stay all night and we don't have enough food, we'll **set you up all night before we'll let you go to bed hungry.**"

Set up housekeeping

Meaning: What a newlywed couple usually does first thing after getting married.

Phrase in use: We're going to move out and get a place and **set up housekeeping** just as soon as we can save up enough money to buy some furniture.

Commentary: Right after the author got married he told his daddy he was going to move out and get a place and **set up**

housekeeping with his new bride, Peggy June. His daddy was shocked and said, "Why Son! What will people think of us if you move out? You're the only son I have or ever will have and folks expect you to keep living with us."

Shake a leg

Meaning: Get a rush on or hurry up.

Phrase in use: Shake a leg kids, you're about to miss the school bus.

Commentary: The children would usually stop and shake one leg and yell, "Look Dad! Look Mom! We're shaking a leg!"

Shake off

Meaning: An expression that the author attributes to his father. A weather related saying meaning it will be dry enough to work when the water falls off the leaves and bushes.

Phrase in use: "Son, it's about quit raining and when it does we'll let it, (meaning bushes, grass, and other forms of vegetation), **shake off** for a while then we'll pick up a helper and go

179

cut another load of acid wood. It's bringing $12.50 a rick now."
Reply, "Okay, if we can cut and load two rick today, I'll take it to
the mill tomorrow when I go to school at TPI." (TPI is now Tennessee Tech.)

Shell down the corn

Meaning: Not relating to corn on the cob, rather, that you should
tell the entire truth about a matter.

Phrase in use: All right Joey, you've caught yourself in a lie so
just go ahead and **shell down the corn.** We know how it hurts
you to tell the truth but it won't kill you just this one time.

Shore

Meaning: Not the seacoast but rather an affirmative response for
"sure."

Phrase in use: "It **shore** is hot ain't it!" That's the way they said it
back then, and many still say **shore** today.

Shucks, doggone, Shucks, Shucks, Shucks

Meaning: A mild expletive.

Phrase in use: A neighbor we called Uncle Henry, although he
was not our uncle, was known to use the expression **shucks doggone** often, while a true uncle, Uncle Shell, would repeat the
expression up to three times in succession for emphasis. **"Shucks
doggone** it, they're trying to raise my taxes again," groaned Uncle

Henry. And upon breaking a plow point on a rock, Uncle Shell would have likely said, **"Shucks! Shucks! Shucks!"** as he surveyed the loss knowing a new one would probably cost a dollar and it would mean making a trip to town before Saturday.

Sinking spell

Meaning: Relating to those people who are weak or often get sick.

Phrase in use: Poor old Uncle Tick had another **sinking spell** last week.

Six of one, half-dozen the other

Meaning: In comparison, both sides are equal.

Phrase in use: "Should we take the bus or ride the mail into town?" Reply, "It makes no difference a'tall, they both cost exactly the same, 10 cents. So it's **six of one, half-dozen the other**."

Skeedadle

Meaning: To hurry or to run.

Phrase in use: "Now you **skeedadle** on down to the spring and bring up a fresh bucket of water."

Skittish

Meaning: A condition of nervousness sometimes referring to animal behavior.

Phrase in use: Better be careful around old Belle. She's kindly **skittish** around strangers.

Slip shucked

Meaning: Leaving another by giving him the slip.

Phrase in use: "We'd better get there early or we'll get **slip shucked** again." Reply, "That's so, why they don't intend to pay the debt they owe us unless we catch them face to face and corner them."

Slow as the seven-year itch

Meaning: Describing a person's gait as being very slow.

Phrase in use: Granddad is as **slow as the seven-year itch** and getting slower every day.

Commentary: The author has never had the **seven-year itch** and hopes he never will, but his sister and he both had the "itch" (scabies) while attending Cedar Grove School during the early 1940s.

The remedy in those days was sulfur and grease applied generously to the entire body. Their mother methodically mixed the compound using grease that had been saved from frying bacon and ham, and then stirred into sulfur. Then the mixture was rubbed into every part of their freshly bathed (with lye soap), bodies that had been scrubbed until the outer layer of skin was almost gone.

Looking back, they now believe that the cure may have been worse than the symptoms suffered from itching and scratching.

Slower than Christmas

Meaning: Particularly for children, the coming of Christmas seems to take an eternity.

Phrase in use: "Child, you'll never get that job finished at the rate you're going because you are **slower than Christmas.** I think maybe a slender limb from that young peach tree might speed you up a bit," mumbled Aunt Jane to herself watching the child piddle at the chore.

Smidgen

Meaning: A very small amount.

Phrase in use: I'll take just a **smidgen** of sugar in my coffee — less than half a teaspoon.

Commentary: A cousin of the author's wife is named Roselyn but has always been called by a nickname, "Midge." It's easy to assume that maybe she was a small child and her nickname could have come from the word in use, **s(midge)n.**

Snag dagget

Meaning: Another mild expletive such as dad gum'mit or dang it. May have been heard in some of the old movies.

Phrase in use: I'll teach that mule a lesson he won't forget, **snag dagget!**

Snooty

Meaning: Referring to someone aloof or reserved in their demeanor and maybe, just a bit snobbish.

Phrase in use: "Miss Carter acts a little **snooty** since she moved back from up north, don't you think?" Reply, "Yes, I met her the other day and she didn't even speak to me. She's just plain stuck-up."

Sodie pop

Meaning: Soft drinks regardless of their trade name.

Phrase in use: I'm going to walk to the store and get me a **sodie pop.**

Commentary: This author usually drank Double Cola or Royal Crown because they came in a 12 oz. bottle rather than the 6 or 8 ounces you got when you bought a Coca Cola. The Nehi drink came in a larger bottle also and in various flavors. NuGrape was another brand in a smaller bottle and then Grapette came along.

It was very tasty but came in a 4 oz. bottle, so seldom did he ever buy one of those.

He clearly remembers that they cost only a nickel each. Inflation has ruined the taste of those wonderful **sodie pops** for him. He only drinks coffee now and says high prices are beginning to hurt the taste of it; however, he still manages to drink a few cups a day.

Somebody's gonna' smell the patching

Meaning: Someone's going to get paid back for doing a wrong.

Phrase in use: Jip sure got the best of me in that mule trade but I guarantee **somebody's gonna' smell the patching** the next time we trade, and it won't be me!

Commentary: The author is unsure where this phrase comes from but it may refer to the glue used to patch inner tubes or other rubber products. There was a hot patch and a cold patch.

In using the hot patch, the glue was spread on and around the leak and a match was struck to light it. It burned for just a few seconds then was blown out creating a terrible smell. Then the patch was placed over the hole and the leak was repaired. It didn't smell good at all so the person doing the repair would certainly be **somebody** who was **gonna' smell the patching.**

Something to remember me by

Meaning: Small token given to a dear friend or lover at parting as a remembrance.

Phrase in use: "Here's **something remember me by.**" Reply, "Thank you, I'll keep it till the day I die."

Song ballet

Meaning: The word "ballad" was intended but regardless the phrase meant a written copy of a song.

Phrase in use: I'd like to have the **song ballet** (lyrics) of that new tune if you can write it out for me.

Commentary: The author recently was reading an issue of *Reminisce* magazine where he saw a reproduction of a Snuffy Smith cartoon in which a friend of Snuffy stated, "I just wrote me a powerful new **song ballet.**" Since the Snuffy character was from Arkansas, the phrase must have been fairly widespread.

Sour milk

Meaning: Buttermilk, the opposite of sweet milk.

Phrase in use: "Do you want sweet milk or sour to drink for supper?" Reply, "I'll take **sour milk** if you have plenty of cornbread."

Commentary: Cornbread and buttermilk were commonly the evening meal, and it was eaten cold thus preventing heating up the house in the summer.

Sparking

Meaning: Romantic relationship with same meaning as "courting."

Phrase in use: "Everyone's talking about how Junior's **sparking** Julie these days." Reply, "They sure are open about it and both seem very happy."

Commentary: The author was reminded of this word after watching an old Eddie Dean movie in which he sang a song entitled "Let's Go **Sparking**". The movie was filmed in 1947. Dean was a great singer and made several movies for PRC, a small company that produced B movies.

Eddie Dean was a protégé of Roy Rogers but never hit the big star status Roy acquired; nonetheless, watching those old black and white pictures is still very enjoyable for many senior citizens, this writer included.

Spazomotic

Meaning: Abnormal behavior such as a "fit."

Phrase in use: A late friend and fellow teacher, Wilbur C. Smith, told the author about how one of his students had insulted him and he threw a "fit" about it. The boy came back to school the next day and addressed his teacher in this manner: "Mr. Smith, you just had a **spazomotic** yesterday, didn't you?"

Spider web stockings and smoking artillery

Meaning: Used to caution one on spending too much.

Phrase in use: This phrase is unique to a single user, the author's father, Booz Garrett, and is included herein as a tribute. Referring to the silk hose and cigarettes his wife, Ove was buying, he admonished her by saying, "Woman, you're going to break me up buying them **spider web stockings and smoking artillery.**" "Break me up" didn't mean that he was going to laugh, but rather he would soon be bankrupt if such frivolous spending continued.

Spizzerringtum

Meaning: Referring to an undisciplined youth.

Phrase in use: That child is a **spizzerringtum** and he'll probably wind up in the penitentiary before he's 21.

Splouze

Meaning: To rush in carelessly and haphazardly, perhaps uninvited.

Phrase in use: "Them kids from up on the mountain **splouzed** through our house after school, went straight to the warming closet, and ate everything I had fixed for supper," the woman said, adding, "then they tracked mud all over my clean floors that just had been scrubbed and mopped, and without a thank you or an apology." Reply, "I know, they do act as though they never had any raising."

Spraddle-legged

Meaning: Walking with your legs spread out.

Phrase in use: She hiked her dress above her knees and went hopping **spraddle-legged** across the mud puddles, not even resembling the little princess her granny pictured her to be. (Oh! Reality can be harsh!)

Commentary: It is truly amazing the way the human mind works. The following incident happened when or before I was three years old and I recall it vividly. I was so young that I was still wetting my pants and when I did I would walk **spraddle-legged** to my mother just as fast as I could go. When we had visitors Mother would tell me to show how I walked when I had wet pants and I would demonstrate by walking **spraddle-legged**. But now, I can't remember something spoken to me ten minutes ago.

Sprag

Meaning: A stick or steel bar used to stop a farm wagon from rolling.

Phrase in use: This plan will work if someone don't throw a **sprag** into it. It could be assumed this method was used in covered wagon days.

Commentary: This word is attributed to a deceased friend, Arnold (Tennessee Slim) Sells, formerly of the Ozone community. It was a wooden stick or iron bar available to be thrown between the spokes of a wagon wheel and the frame to serve as a brake or to keep it from rolling. It was usually applied when travelling uphill with a heavy load if the mules stalled and the wagon began to roll backwards.

Stand up and take your medicine

Meaning: Sometimes referred to taking something that would help you but more often meaning you were about to get a spanking, paddling, or a good switching — so just stand up and take it.

Phrase in use: The teacher caught Junior pulling Lois' hair and ordered him to "just **stand up and take your medicine**," because he was caught red-handed.

Commentary: On the subject of medicine, those most often used around our house were castor oil, Epsom salts, and Black Drought for internal ailments. The most prominent rub-on remedy was the aforementioned, sulfur and grease. In every case, the remedy was much worse than the symptoms, or at least that's what we children believed.

Step-ins

Meaning: That's what undergarments worn by females were called and youngsters were forbidden to say in the presence of mixed company.

Phrase in use: "I saw Suzy's **step-ins** when she climbed the tree last recess." Reply, "You better not tell or you'll get a paddling from the teacher, and another one from your parents when you get home."

Stiffer'n a chicken, Stiffer'n a board

Meaning: Emphasizing the degree of stiffness in an object.

Phrase in use: Our old cow that died last week was **stiffer'n a chicken** by the time we found her.

Sti't

Meaning: This phrase is unique to Shelton Robbins, my brother-in-law. The word is a contraction combining the words "still" and "yet" and its meaning is best demonstrated by the usage example.

Phrase in use: "The beans we planted **sti't** didn't come up," moaned Shelton after the extended cold spell this spring.

Store bought

Meaning: Anything purchased at a store and not homemade.

Phrase in use: Our cousin from Chicago wears only **store bought** clothes.

Story

Meaning: A lie.

Phrase in use: "Now children, you'd better not **story** to me because I'll wear you out if you do. You know the old saying, *the truth hurts*, but there are things that may hurt worse. Can you hear me now?" The children need not reply to the question, they heard it loud and clear.

Stove up

Meaning: Referring to something being forced inward as when a ball hits you on the end of the finger.

Phrase in use: "Joab's still all **stove up** from falling out of the persimmon tree last Saturday night." Reply, "Yep! The 'possum stayed in the tree while Joab hit the ground on his head." (Ever see a 'possum grin? Well, that one did.)

Strike out

Meaning: Not relating to baseball here but rather a phrase meaning to leave immediately.

Phrase in use: "Daddy, Mother said we could meet the Ray girls at their spring and play 'til sundown if you don't care." Reply, "**Strike out!** But you better be home before dark. You know the copperheads are crawling everywhere after sundown this time of year, and we'll wear you out if you come in here snakebit."

Strip-stark naked

Meaning: Wearing no clothing.

Phrase in use: The story goes that a young man said that his little brother came into a room full of company and that he would have been **strip-stark naked** if he hadn't been wearing a wrist watch. Some might have remarked, "He was **naked as a picked bird.**"

Struttin' like a big, fat patterge

Meaning: A bird, the Partridge.

Phrase in use: "Have you seen Eli since he got married?" Reply, "Yeah, he was in town Saturday with his new bride and they were both **struttin' like a big, fat patterge.**"

Commentary: These birds are seldom seen in these parts now but were once here in abundance. The phrase originated from the way they walk with their heads high and in sort of a strut. Partridges nested on the ground and if you were walking alone in the dark and startled a flock they would all fly up at the same time causing a great "swooshing" sound that would just about scare you to death.

Stuck up

Meaning: People who are conceited, snobbish, or snooty.

Phrase in use: "Thelma Jean is a little bit **stuck up** since she came back from Las Vegas." Reply, "Why I met her at church last week and she wouldn't even speak to me. Acted like she didn't even know me. The very likes of her, wearing that big diamond ring and fine clothes! She was as poor as Job's turkey before she left here and my opinion is that she struck a rich, old, gold mine.

Suck-egg dog

Meaning: A dog with a very bad habit, he sucked eggs.

Phrase in use: "Del accused old General of sucking a dozen eggs last night and threatened to shoot him." Reply, "He did it to, but Art still denies that he owns a **suck-egg dog.**"

Commentary: A suck-egg dog was despised by everyone in the community except his owner who would always deny any wrong-doing by the scoundrel. Chickens were a valuable asset and when a hen's nest got "broke up" by a **suck-egg dog**, it could not be tolerated.

Suit of clothes

Meaning: A suit was referred to in this manner. Came to be called a suit of clothes because a suit was almost always multiple pieced.

Phrase in use: Richard just bought a new **suit of clothes.**

Sum'mers

Meaning: Somewhere.

Phrase in use: They used to live **sum'mers** up around Cincinnati before they moved back down here.

Sun grins

Meaning: The silly smile made when facing the bright sun.

Phrase in use: "Every time I have my picture took, I get the **sun grins**," giggled little Sissy. Reply from Kim, "That's the truth, you sure looked silly in last year's school picture."

Commentary: When they had their pictures made it was a standing rule that you had to be facing the sun so it's possible that could be the origin of this phrase.

Sunday-go-to-meetin' clothes

SUNDAY BEST

Meaning: Dressed in your very best clothes.

Phrase in use: You kids sure look nice all dressed up in your **Sunday-go- to-meetin' clothes.**

Commentary: The author remembers as a boy seeing the older men of the community dressed in their **Sunday-go-to-meetin' clothes** for funerals and sometimes to go to church. This attire usually consisted of brand new or freshly washed and starched overalls, a neatly starched and ironed white shirt, and a necktie tucked down behind the overalls' bib. This was considered standard dress for the men folks on such occasions. Many of the women and girls wore dresses that were made from material called "print" or one made from a feed sack.

Sup, Swaller

Meaning: Describing a small sip (sup) and a long, large drink (swaller). Better just take a **sup** until you find out what you're drinking. You might just wake up in the middle of tomorrow.

Phrase in use: Sup was usually preceded by the word "little" whereas **swaller** was almost always preceded by the word "big." Example: "Jim, you can have a little **sup** of this moonshine, and Comer, you can have a big **swaller.**"

Surp

Meaning: Their word for "syrup," that sweet, sticky liquid poured over pancakes or spread on a hot, buttered biscuit.

Phrase in use: Them buttered pancakes covered with hot maple **surp** shore were good eat'n.

Sweet mash

Meaning: A pile-on game they played in Elementary School.

Phrase in use: When someone fell down another would yell **sweet mash** and everyone within the sound of his voice piled on top of him, sometimes eight or ten. It was great fun for those on top, but pure misery for those poor souls whose lot it fell to be on the bottom. The game was sometimes referred to as **free mash.**

Sweetening

Meaning: Dessert.

Phrase in use: Do you have any **sweetening** to go with this ham?

Swivet

Meaning: A word suggesting you not get nervous and upset over small things.

Phrase in use: Now don't get yourself in a **swivet** over this because it may not be as bad as it seems. Just lay low 'till we learn the truth of the matter and then it can be dealt with in a rational manner.

Commentary: Oftentimes bad decisions are made because we react on impulse or jump to quick solutions without waiting to hear all the facts of the matter. This happens when we allow ourselves to get in a **swivet**.

T

Take it out in trade

Meaning: A method of debt settlement.

Phrase in use: The customer asked the storekeeper, "Do you want to pay me for the potatoes now or wait until the end of the week?" Reply, "I'll be having you to work some for me soon so you could settle the bill by **taking it out in trade.**"

Commentary: This was a common method of payment when general store owners and "truck croppers" did business.

Taking my own good time

Meaning: Accomplishing something but at a slow pace.

Phrase in use: Because they were **taking their own good time** in doing the chores, they all got a good whuppin'.

Commentary: The author is reminded about a story involving his great aunt Sade. She lined her children up one morning and gave them all a sound whuppin'. When they protested that they hadn't done anything wrong, she told them they probably would before the day was over and whipped them anyway.

She's also the one who told her husband she hoped she'd never see him again as he left to go work in the log woods. She got her wish. A tree fell on him and killed him and he never got back home.

Taking on

Meaning: Not adding to but rather something entirely different. It meant to wail, moan, or cry loudly.

Phrase in use: They were screaming and **taking on** like a family member had died when their old fox hound that had been missing so long a time turned up dead.

Tend to your own knittin'

Meaning: Keep your nose out of my business.

Phrase in use: Hank Williams said it best in one of his songs, "If you mind your own business then you won't be minding mine." Of course, he could have written, "If you **tend to your own knittin'** then you won't be tending to mine." Somehow, though, it's doubtful that would have sold many records.

Thanks 'till you're better paid

Meaning: Thanks for not charging me for your labor.

Phrase in use: "Well, **thanks 'til you're better paid.**" Then the reply might be, "Just charge it to the ground and let the rain settle it."

That give me out

Meaning: Simply put, it made me tired.

Phrase in use: Lifting all those heavy boxes **that give me out.**

That beats a goose a' rootin'

Meaning: Showing surprise or shock.

Phrase in use: "Art and Dellie finally jumped the broom," Ona V. stated. Thurman's reply, "Well! **That beats a goose a rootin'!** They've been sparking for twenty-odd years."

That's all she wrote

Meaning: Statement finalizing an issue.

Phrase in use: He packed up his bags and left and **that's all she wrote.**

That's a new one on me

Meaning: Learning or hearing something for the first time.

Phrase in use: "They say your neighbor run off with his second cousin and got married." Reply, "I do declare, **that's a new one on me!**"

That's a new wrinkle on my horn

Meaning: Response to hearing or learning something new.

Phrase in use: "Did you know they have invented a car tire that has no tube?" Reply, "**That's a new wrinkle on my horn.**"

That's it

Meaning: Words of agreement or completion.

Phrase in use: Thanks to a friend, Willie Bilbrey, for his recollection of the usage of this phrase: "I just thought of Granny Smith's first name, it was 'Callie.'" Reply, **"That's it**! I remember now." Another usage, "Well, **that's it**! I'll never trust him again since he's lied to me twice!"

That's just an old Eddards' saying

Meaning: Speculated origin of statements.

Phrase in use: Whimpered poor Faye, "I know it's going to rain 'cause all my joints are hurting."

Lura's reply, "Unlikely! Don't you know **that's just an old Eddards' saying?**"

Commentary: Lura Gray heard this phrase when she was young and it probably referred to a family named Edwards. Many people pronounced the name Edwards as "Eddards." That's what Lum Edwards of the famous radio duo Lum and Abner called himself. He always introduced himself as Lum Eddards. Abner's last name was Peabody and they owned the  Jot 'em down store, library, bakery, and museum in the fictitious town of Pine Ridge, Arkansas.

The bighead

Meaning: Being conceited or "stuck up."

Phrase in use: "The Carter family seems to have gotten **the bighead** since they moved up north." Reply, "They act just plum stuck up and snooty if you're asking me."

The shoe's on the other foot now

Meaning: A shift in positions of power.

Phrase in use: "We finally got our man elected Sheriff." Reply, "Yeah and the bootleggers better watch out 'cause **the shoe's on the other foot now.**"

The worm has turned

Meaning: The weaker one has turned, and instead of running, has taken a stand against the stronger one.

Phrase in use: "Little Billy finally had enough of Jack's bullying and beat the stuffing out of him." Reply, "Yes, **the worm has turned.**"

They jumped the broom

Meaning: They got married.

Phrase in use: "Did you hear about Ed and Peg? **They jumped the broom** last night." Reply, "You mean they just up and ran off and got married?"

They'll charge an arm and a leg

Meaning: Whatever you're buying will be extremely expensive.

Phrase in use: "You'd better not eat at that new place that just opened. **They'll charge an arm and a leg.**" Heard in reply, "You'd better believe it! We ate there one time and a hamburger cost 75 cents and coffee 20 cents a cup. They can't expect poor folks to pay those prices."

Thicker'n hops

Meaning: Strong relationship between people.

Phrase in use: "The Browns and the Smiths have become really close friends since the campaign for mayor started last week. Reply, "I'd say they're **thicker'n hops** or just like two peas in a pod, and my friend, that's too close."

This world and one more and then the fireworks

Meaning: Expression used after hearing something shocking or surprising.

Phrase in use: "Did you hear about the bill that Congress just passed that is sure to ruin the workingman?" Reply, "Well I swan! **This world and one more and then the fireworks!**"

Three moving's equal a burnout

Meaning: A very old expression meaning that when you move you throw away or leave behind a lot of your possessions. So, after moving three times, there's not much left.

Phrase in use: They felt that three moving's (changing your residence three times) represented a loss of possessions of the same magnitude as having your house burn down with everything in it. It makes sense then, that **three moving's equal a burn out.**

Three shakes of a sheep's tail

Meaning: To happen quickly.

Phrase in use: Quoting Nimrod, "Just hold on a minute, I'll be there in **three shakes of a sheep's tail." Or, "In three shakes of a dead sheep's tail,"** meaning not hardly as fast.

Three sheets in the wind

Meaning: Heavy drinking or being drunk.

Phrase in use: Hacklett was about **three sheets in the wind** last night and he'll probably be that way for three weeks.

Commentary: No clue as to the origin of this saying.

Throw knives

Meaning: The act of trading knives.

Phrase in use: "Want to **throw knives** today?" asked Cleston. Replied J.B., "No, I like my old Case and I think I'll just keep it for a while."

Thumb a ride

Meaning: Hitchhiking.

Phrase in use: "Let's meet at Leck's barn, **thumb a ride** to town, and see the movie next Saturday." "I'll be there," said Doak in agreement.

Tide me over

Meaning: Just enough to get by on.

Phrase in use: Billie remarked, "I didn't eat much breakfast today — just enough to **tide me over** 'till dinner." Monty answered, "Well, let's go eat now."

Tight as Dick's hatband

Meaning: Something that fits tightly.

Phrase in use: "My new shoes feel as **tight as Dick's hatband**." Nothing more is known about Dick or his hatband but it made him somewhat famous. Could this be the same Dick that went in the Army lighting his pipe and came out smoking it? Or maybe he's the one who hangs out with Tom and Harry?

To beat the band

Meaning: Being completely involved in an activity.

Phrase in use: Those children were having a great time and jumping the rope just **to beat the band.**

Too short in the britch

Meaning: A way of telling a child that he is too small or too young for a job.

Phrase in use: Searching for an example of usage brings to mind a story that has been told about the author for as long as he can remember. Although not more than three years old, he can remember specific details from this encounter. He has put his memories into rhyme to tell this true story...

...The Wade Escapade

T'was an odd couple there on that hot summer day, a man and a boy who was just in the way, the man was at work, the toddler at play had been left in the care of the worker Wade Ray.

There were holes to be dug in the red clay and chert, and a fence to be nailed to the posts in the dirt, and all the while seeing the boy didn't get hurt, little Eddie was tugging on Wade's sweat-drenched shirt.

*Said I want to dig, placed his hand on the digger, you'll have to wait till you're a little bit bigger, **too short in the britch** right now I figure, insulted the boy took off in a dither.*

Down past the woodshed and smokehouse he stalked, huffing and puffing on down the stone walk, in through the front door and down to the hall, his lips in a pout, he leaned back on the wall.

My darling! My darling! Mother Ove cried out, what in the world has brought on this pout? Tell me my baby, what's this all about! And she lifted her Eddie Boy onto her lap.

It's that old Wade Ray, my daddy's own cousin, I wanted to dig but he started cussin', called me two son-of-a-bitches while he was fussin', tears of self-pity from the boy's eyes came gushing.

Wade came in for dinner, the mother was riled, he heard the story and started to smile, then he explained what he'd said to the child, and a folk tale was born that would last a long while.

Is this story true? Yes! I do declare! With a few words of color thrown in here and there, taking poetic license just to give it a flair, but the boy heard those cuss words, I know I was there!

(Editor's note: Every character and place in this poem is real and in my mind I can see them, almost as clearly today as then. If Wade was still living, he would verify every detail of this incident.)

* * *

Tol'ble

Meaning: Shortened version of the word "tolerable." Some pronounced it **tola'ble**. There was one old gentleman the author knew who never replied with **tol'ble**. His reply was always, "Ordinary, just ordinary."

Phrase in use: "How you feeling today?" Reply, "Oh, **tol'ble** I guess."

Tom sop

Meaning: Another name for white gravy.

Phrase in use: Pass the **tom sop**, please.

Commentary: **Tom sop** was the name for white gray or the 'thicken' gravy they ate for breakfast daily. It was delicious with bacon, sausage, country ham, and biscuits. A typical breakfast for the author consisted of the items aforementioned plus red gravy, if they had country ham, and of course honey or molasses.

On certain occasions, his mother would catch a pullet, (that's a frying chicken), dress it, and fry it for breakfast. Sometimes the offering would include fried corn and sweet potatoes.

The red gravy mentioned is made by using the grease from the fried country ham and cooking it with water. Some cooks used coffee rather than water. It's about the same as what we are served in restaurants today called "Au jou" but it certainly tasted better.

Too fur and snakey

Meaning: Great distance and hazardous.

Phrase in use: "I'm going to California. Want to go with me?" "No!" "Why?" "**Too fur and snakey**." **Fur** means "far" and **snakey** is "hazardous."

Tooter

Meaning: An unruly child or a young woman who was a little "fast."

Phrase in use: She's a **Tooter** but she sure is a cute little thing. Her parents are to blame. They let her do as she pleases and never correct her.

Tough as whitleather

Meaning: In reference to how tough something or someone might be. "Whitleather," as it turns out, is leather, often goatskin, that has been tanned and treated with alum and salt. That process not only lightens the color of the leather, but also renders it soft and pliable, yet very strong and tough, making it a popular material for straps and thongs. Whitleather also used to be known as "alum leather" and "Hungarian leather," and a tanner who made whitleather was known as a "whittawer," the archaic verb "to taw" meaning (what else?) "to prepare leather by steeping in alum and salt."

Phrase in use: "You'd better leave that boy alone, he's as **tough as whitleather** and he'll whup the pants off'n you if you start an argument with him. You'd best remember, he does his arguing with his fists."

Trading daylight for dark

Meaning: Wasting valuable daylight time, and having to finish the job in the dark.

Phrase in use: The men were advised to work a little faster or they'd be **trading daylight for dark.**

Truck patches

Meaning: Small plots of land where garden vegetables were grown to be peddled or sold from truck beds or roadside stands.

Phrase in use: "You plan on raising a big crop this year?" Reply, "No, just a garden and a few **truck patches** is about all."

Commentary: Many farmers and even sharecroppers grew beans, potatoes, tomatoes, corn, and melons to be trucked to the "big road" or on into town to be sold to grocers, other peddlers, or individuals who liked the freshly grown produce.

Turn

Meaning: Two uses, first describing ones personality and second, a volume of corn.

Phrase in use: First: Sally Rose was the most popular girl in school and because she had a good **turn** everyone liked her. Second: A **turn** of corn was whatever amount you could get in a tow sack, usually a bushel or more, the exact amount did not matter.

Commentary: One was careful not to fill the corn sack too full. They tried to make it balance just across the withers of the mule or horse so it wouldn't slide off when the animal walked. When taken by mule, they'd often go down Mill Creek to Uncle L. Bilbrey's watermill and wait while he ground the corn into meal. Those millers seldom charged money for their work but took a "toll" (a small portion) from your meal.

Turn you across my checked apron

Meaning: Impending spanking or switching.

Phrase in use: Better watch it kid or, I'll **turn you across my checked apron**.

Commentary: Northerners say "**checkered apron**" but we know they all talk funny. The daddies used this phrase too, although none were ever known to wear **checked aprons**.

Two heads are better than one, and sometimes added, even if one is a blockhead

Meaning: Two opinions are better than one.

Phrase in use: "Thanks for your opinion about how to price my bull; **two heads are** always **better than one.**" Reply, "That's true, **even if one is a blockhead.**" (To which of the two "blockhead" referred, no one knows.)

Two peas in a pod

Meaning: Expressing a close relationship between two people.

Phrase in use: The Smiths and Lees are closer than **two peas in a pod**.

Two wrongs don't make a right

Meaning: Don't do something wrong to atone for a previous mistake.

Phrase in use: "He stole money to pay for the damages he had done when his mules ran through the old man's fence." Reply, "He'll have to learn that **two wrongs don't make a right.**"

U

Ugly as a mud fence and daubed as a tadpole

Meaning: Boys commenting about certain girls.

Phrase in use: "How ugly is that new girl?" Reply, **"Ugly as a mud fence and daubed as a tadpole."**

Commentary: Of course there weren't any ugly girls in our school, or at least that's what we younger boys thought. Wasn't it strange that the older girls were so much prettier than those our age when we were just boys, and even stranger was how quickly they became so beautiful just two years later.

Ugly as homemade sin

Meaning: Boy's comment about certain girls or their mothers.

Phrase in use: "How ugly is her mother?" Reply, **"Ugly as homemade sin."**

Under the weather

Meaning: Expression describing health meaning same as "poorly," "ailing," or just plain sick to the point of being plum "down."

Phrase in use: "How are you today, Uncle Rob?" Reply, "Not too good, I've been **under the weather** here of late."

Up and left

Meaning: Leaving the scene suddenly.

Phrase in use: "That young girl old Brassel married while he was in Reno just **up and left** last week." Reply, "Yep! The rumor is she's gone back west but others say she's still around here."

Up the creek without a paddle

Meaning: In a desperate situation.

Phrase in use: Dock stated, "Boys we've run out of gas right here in the middle of nowhere." Bill replied, "Yeah, I guess we're just **up the creek without a paddle.**"

U'rn

Meaning: Pronounced the same as "urn," a container, but they meant "ours."

Phrase in use: Them ain't your pencils, they're **u'rn**, so give them back, and don't try to steal them again!

Commentary: How strange it seems now that those quaint words in the above phrase were commonly used when the author was a small boy many years ago but are never heard now.

Edwin Garrett

V

Vie'grus

Meaning: Correctly pronounced by rhyming with "tigerus." Thought to be the same as vigorous as no other word was found with which to relate it.

Phrase in use: You'd better watch that dog, he has a **vie'grus** bark. (Sounds like he may have a **vie'gru**s bite, too.)

W

Walk the chalk

Meaning: You'd better behave yourself and stay in line.

Phrase in use: "You children had better **walk the chalk** Sunday when the preacher comes for dinner or I'll tan your leather."
Reply, "We'll be good 'cause we shore don't want no whuppin'."

Well children

Meaning: An expression used in showing surprise.

Phrase in use: "Did you hear about the big fight last night after church?" Reply, **"Well children!** What will those Deacons do next?"

Commentary: Isabel (Buford) Garrett says, **"Well child!** I never heard tell of such!" Both mean the same. Mrs. Isabel, also lovingly known as Granny Garrett by her many former students and fellow teachers is now 101 years old. A lifelong school teacher she kept working as a substitute into her 98th year, about the same time she gave up driving.

Well I'll be John Brown

Meaning: Another phrase showing surprise. Speculated that this phrase refers to the **John Brown** whose body… "lies sleeping in his grave."

Phrase in use: "Did you know Albert died out last night?" Reply, **"Well I'll be John Brown**! I thought he'd live to be at least a hundred years old."

Well I swan, Well I swanee

Meaning: Spoken by those surprised or amazed.

Phrase in use: "**Well I swan!** The pie supper at Timothy last week brought in $11 for the purchase of pencils and paper and other school supplies for those students that have no money for such," said Geneva. Dalton's reply, **"Well, I swanee**, ain't that good!"

Well off

Meaning: Financially secure.

Phrase in use: Most of the farmers around Willow Grove were **well off** when the big dam was built, but they had to leave their good farms and move to higher ground.

Watch after

Meaning: To take care of such as children or sheep.

Phrase in use: The author's father would often tell the rest of the family to **watch after** things if he was late getting in from the stock sale. **Watch after** also meant to do up the "night work" before dark.

Waylaid

Meaning: Ambushed.

Phrase in use: The Renshaw boys **waylaid** young Jamesion, caught him when he was by himself, and beat him up because he had been trying to court their sister.

Commentary: The only reason they could give for the ambush was that they didn't want their sister a courtin' no Republican. Some believed, however, that the real reason was that the young man was a Methodist.

We'll hang you up on a nail

Meaning: The same as saying, we'll make a place for you somehow if you want to stay all night.

Phrase in use: Aw, y'all don't have to leave now, **we'll hang you up on a nail** if you'll stay all night with us.

Went right off without it

*Oh no!
I forgot something...
But what?*

Meaning: Just forgot it.

Phrase in use: "Mother had our school lunch all fixed and I was in a hurry and **went right off without it.** Heck! That eight pound lard bucket was packed full of cornbread, butterbeans, and ham meat, but we don't have time to go back and get it now. We'll be late for school if we do."

What'd you come for, a coal of fire?

Meaning: An expression used when a visitor could only stay for a few minutes.

Phrase in use: What'd you come for, a coal of fire? Why don't you stay and visit for a few minutes?

Commentary: An incident is recalled by the author of a time when he was in school at Cedar Grove during WWII. The teacher that year was from another community and rented a large room in the Uncle Shell Burgess house, which the Jackson family had leased. They were living in another part of the large dwelling.

Mrs. Vassie came to school and began class one morning by asking the students to guess what she had borrowed from the Jacksons that morning. They guessed sugar, coffee, flour, butter, eggs, and every food item they could think of but none were the right answer. Finally, when they were out of guesses, she gave them the answer, "fire."

The house had a large fireplace on each end of the building and that was the source of heat during winter. The teacher had let her fire go out during the night and was out of matches so she just went into the next room and borrowed some fire coals.

This was a good method of creating interest and instigating discussion among the students, and without a doubt the indication of a good teacher. Interestingly, this was a one-room school so Mrs. Vassie was both principal and teacher of grades 1-8.

What'd you 'low

Meaning: What is your opinion of the matter, or what do you allow? (Rhyme 'low with "cow" for the proper sound.)

Phrase in use: I think the war will end soon, **what'd you 'low?**

When I get my rich uncle out of the poor house

Meaning: I'll do big things when I get rich.

Phrase in use: "What do you think of Ozzie's new car?" Reply, "I'll have me one just like it **when I get my rich uncle out of the poor house.**"

Whipstitch

Meaning: Frequent action.

227

Phrase in use: The neighbors drop in on Grandpa just every little **whipstitch** since he's been ailing, and this kind gesture is appreciated by all.

White-eye

Meaning: A quitter, starting something but never finishing. Most commonly referring to a lazy person.

Phrase in use: The boy Mr. Barlow hired to chop out his corn **white-eyed** before he got through the first row.

Why shore, by crackies

Meaning: Expressing assurance or satisfaction.

Phrase in use: One among many **by**-words such as, by jacks, by jingo, by hoakies, by gum, by gar, by gosh, by heck, by doggies, by Ned, by golly, and on and on. ("**Why shore! By crackies!** That shore is a lot of **by**-words.")

Wilder than a co-op rat

Meaning: Phrase used for comparison, such as a rat that infests a Farmer's Co-operative grain barn.

Phrase in use: The Rayburns can't do a thing with that boy of theirs 'cause he's **wilder'n a co-op rat.**

Won't last as long as a June frost
Meaning: A very short time.

Phrase in use: My mother knew my mad spell **wouldn't last as long as a June frost** and that I'd get in a good mood right quick when I smelled that country ham frying.

Work brickel

Meaning: One who is lazy and not at all eager to do any sort of work especially hard labor.

Phrase in use: Mr. England didn't think the boy was very **work brickle** after he quit the first day.

Wosper

Meaning: A wasp, a relative to a hornet.

Phrase in use: A big, red **wosper** stung Ralph right betwixt his eyes.

Wouldn't be in his shoes for his socks

Meaning: Referring to a person who is in a bad situation or maybe in trouble with the law.

Phrase in use: "Young Scott's sure got hisself in a mess of trouble this time." Reply, "Yeah boy! I **wouldn't be in his shoes for his socks!** He's headed for a stay in the Crossbar Hotel!"

Wouldn't work in a pie factory

Meaning: Referring to a lazy person.

Phrase in use: Everybody around here says Homer is so lazy he **wouldn't work in a pie factory** even if they changed flavors every fifteen minutes.

Commentary: Long years ago a man left these parts and was gone for a year. When he returned he said he had been working in a banana factory but that he quit the job because sticking the skins on the banana cob was just too hard.

XYZ

Yaller

Meaning: They meant "yellow."

Phrase in use: That old boy's got a **yaller** streak down his back a yard wide, and if he don't learn to keep his smart mouth shut he'll be running a long time. It's a known fact that he's not going to stand up and fight.

Yard sale-ing

Meaning: A relatively new expression enjoying frequent usage. It refers to one who often attends yard sales.

Phrase in use: Ronnie stated, "Bobbie will surely wear out her new car going **yard sale-ing** so much." Replied her twin sister Carol, "That's the truth. Why, she ain't missed a one in nigh on two years now. Her neighbor says she's either going to one or just returning with a load, or she's getting ready to have her own yard sale."

Yeah-huh

Meaning: A special and unique communication to mother. This saying is attributed to the late Cloise Staggs.

Phrase in use: According to Jerry Hall, Cloise would always say to his mother, "**Yeah-huh**, Ma, we'd better be getting in home. If we leave right now, it'll be sundown again' we get there and it'll be good dark before I can get all my hound dogs fed and shut up." (Cloise loved his dogs.)

Yea-hoo

Meaning: Pronounced "yay-who" and referring to a stranger or an undesirable person about whom very little was known. They were suspicious of any outsider or anyone who might have been "from off from here."

Phrase in use: "Who was that **yea-hoo** who kept flirting with my girlfriend?" Reply, "I don't know but I hope he don't plan to be here long. He seems to have a way with all the girls."

Yep, Nope

Meaning: Yes and No.

Phrase in use: **Yep** is a version of the affirmative, "yes" and **nope** means, "no."

You all, Y'all

Meaning: More than one person or all of you.

Phrase in use: In the Bible, Job 17:10, Job in his reply to his miserable comforters said, "But as for **you all**, do ye return and come now; for I cannot find one wise man among you."

Commentary: Those unfamiliar with Southern language and customs think "you all" meant one person, but to those from the South, the term has always spoken of more than one, the same as did Job's **you all**. Some shorten it more to, **y'all.**

You can't beat that with a kraut maul

Meaning: Descriptive of something that really worked well or something that was very good.

Phrase in use: I told you that would work well, why **you can't beat that with a kraut maul.**

Commentary: This phrase is unique to my friend the late Arnold Sells from the Taylor's Crossroads Community. I met Arnold (Tennessee Slim) in Akron, Ohio in 1956 and we played in the same band until I left there in 1961.

You'll do great wonders and eat raw cucumbers

Meaning: A retaliation used to counter a threat preceding a fight.

Phrase in use: "If you don't shut your mouth, I'll knock the Joe Sorrels outt'a you." Reply, "Yeah, you and whose army? **You'll do great wonders and eat raw cucumbers**! That's all you will do!"

Commentary: The author is reminded of an incident that happened when he was a student in elementary school many years ago, described below. The Mayflower Compact was written just before the Pilgrims landed at Plymouth Rock. It was a guide for social and governmental structure for the new land, and it served its purpose well. Another such agreement, the Cedar Grove Compact, also served to keep peace in a tiny one-room school, even if it only lasted for less than one day it became known to a few as…

…The Cedar Grove Compact

Trouble was astir at the Cedar Grove School. Big trouble! It was morning's recess around the year of 1944 and WWII was still raging. But another war, although a much smaller one, was about to break out on this fine spring day. Unbeknownst to the teacher, she was the source of the trouble that was just about to erupt.

She was young and beautiful, and just completing her high school education. She had been hired to finish out the school-year because teachers were scarce at that time. We seldom had the same teacher all year long, because all the men had gone off to war and many of the women had gone North to work in the defense factories.

Because of this, high school students often served as our teachers. Some had already graduated while others just took leave in order to earn a little money.

Getting back to the Compact: Teddy, Odus, and I were all in love with the same woman, the teacher, Miss Peterman. Oh! She was a beauty and each of us "claimed" her as our sweetheart.

Being the oldest of the three I believed that I had the inside track. I reasoned that Teddy was just too young for her and that I was much better looking than Odus. But, nonetheless, the problem still existed, and tension surrounded the three of us as we finally began to argue about it.

"She's my girl!" Odus firmly stated.

"That's not so!" retorted Teddy angrily. "She likes me much better than she does either one of you boys!"

"You're both wrong!" I snapped. "Everyone in school knows she's crazy about me!"

The fight was ready to begin. Fists were clenched, faces were red with anger, except for Odus who was white as a ghost, and knees atremble when, with a wisdom far beyond his young years, Odus had a solution that would save the friendships and retain peace at the Cedar Grove School.

His solution was a simple one: "Let's just all quit her," he said, "I'll quit her right now if you boys will!"

Well, that seemed like a good idea and would surely save a fight. *Why hadn't I thought of that?* Anyway, I hadn't hardly figured out how we were all three going to fight at one time, seeing that Teddy and I were first cousins and would probably take sides against Odus. He may have been thinking that too when he came up with his brilliant idea.

Yes, his plan made a lot of sense. I said I'd go along with it and Teddy agreed also. "You boys want to shake on it?" Odus asked.

We both agreed, we all three shook hands, and the Cedar Grove Compact was sealed without ever being written down on paper or recorded in any official government office. It was short-lived, however, because by evening's recess we were all three tagging around after the teacher and bickering behind her back about who she liked best.

I still wonder to this day if she ever knew she was the center of all that controversy. (Ah! Young love! How sweet it was!)

Yourn'zes

Meaning: It belongs to you, or you all, it's not ours.

Phrase in use: "Wait a minute boys, we've got to divide these hick'ery nuts we've picked up." Reply, "No, we've already got u'rn, them's all **your'nzes**." A more modern way to express it, "We have ours, those are yours." You may ask if they really did talk that way." 'Tis true! I know, I was there! However, it was a long, long time ago.

You've got the case

Meaning: The decision is yours.

Phrase in use: "Do whatever you think is right," or as G.P. would say, **"you've got the case, son."**

Young'uns

Meaning: Referring to children and young adults.

Phrase in use: You **young'uns** better be sure to wash your feet before getting into Grannie's clean bed.

Your'n

Meaning: Belonging to you exclusively.

Phrase in use: The little one is **your'n** (yours) 'cause u'rn (ours) is much bigger.

Yours

Meaning: This was Aunt Margie's way of replying to a "thank you" from someone instead of the traditional phrase "You're welcome."

Phrase in use: "I thank you for the candy, Aunt Margie. It sure was good." Reply, **"Yours."**

Commentary: Now instead of "you're welcome" we hear "no problem," or "no prob."

You won't need any help to catch him but you may need some help to turn him loose

Meaning: The meaning is best explained through its usage below.

Phrase in use: **You won't need any help to catch him but you may need some help to turn him loose** meaning, easy to catch but hard to let go. The following commentary relates one incident I remember vividly when "Tapper" Tom said it to try to prevent Cousin Billy from being hurt.

Commentary: Billy, "Tapper" Tom, and I were crossing the little field just above the Cedar thicket when Billy's dog, Butch, and my two dogs, Brownie and George, began leaping high above the hay because they had "jumped" something, probably a rabbit we thought.

The chase was brief because whatever they were chasing quickly found refuge under a small but shallow opening beneath a tiny rock ledge. The three of us followed the dogs as fast as we could but never got a glimpse of the varmint.

When we got to the hole, Billy got down on his hands and knees trying to see what was hiding there. All three dogs were barking fiercely because they wanted the world to know they had something treed. They probably knew what it was and Billy thought he knew too.

"He rabbit!" he yelled excitedly. "I'm going to reach in the hole and see if I can catch him!"

"Tapper" Tom was not so sure and warned Billy that it might be a ground hog. "If it is a ground hog, **you won't need any help to catch him, but you may need some help to turn him loose,**" "Tapper" Tom cautioned using his favorite saying.

Anyway, Billy reached far back into the den and immediately began screaming with pain and trying to pull his hand out. A great tussle ensued and finally Billy's hand came out with a large ground hog's teeth attached to the skin between the first finger and thumb. Of course the teeth were also attached to the animal.

"He ground hog! He ground hog!" cried little Billy. It took a good while and some hard choking by Tom to finally get the boy's hand free. By then, Billy's trophy "rabbit" was done in for good. The moral of the story is exactly as "Tapper" Tom stated: *Billy* **didn't need any help to catch him but he did need some help to turn him loose.**

Epilogue and Acknowledgements

L ooking back now, as this book comes to completion, one of the greatest problems I have encountered is bringing it to an end. My advisor kept saying, "Don't add any more words." But, it never seemed to end. Additional sayings and by-words of old kept popping into my mind and I could not resist the urge to add "just one more."

I mention this merely as a clue that there will probably be another book coming; that is, if time allows me the strength and days of life to complete it. There are already many more old sayings and by-words at the top of my memory bank, ready to spring onto the computer screen.

I would be remiss if I failed to mention those persons who have been a part of this endeavor. First of all, my wife, Peggy, and our three children, Kim, Marty (Lounetta), and Lisa and husband, Chris Coil. My sister, Ann Maxine Nivens, who in her own right is a published author and poet, along with several members of her family who have encouraged and submitted or reminded me of words and phrases.

And finally in this elite group, Cousin Charles Burgess of Greenwood, Indiana, who is a prolific writer himself, having had at least three books, and numerous newspaper articles and stories published. He has been so much a part of this writing that he should be listed as a co-writer. He labored under great duress and never became discouraged or impatient with me, and his computer skills were invaluable.

I am forever indebted to each member of this group for their help, encouragement, and patience. They each deserve much of the credit or blame, however this may turn out. Just kidding. All the blame for any shortcomings in this effort are accredited entirely to me.

Many other friends, former students, fellow teachers, and acquaintances, have come forward with reminders of by-words that I had never heard or had forgotten. They deserve to be mentioned and their names follow, or as many as I can remember. You see, I failed to keep a listing of those who provided words, so let's hope that my memory serves me well.

Contributors

Peggy Garrett, Charles England, Willie Hugh Bilbrey, Sheldon Barlow, Ralph Barlow, Jeff Barlow, Pat Poston, Lura Gray via Pat Poston, Sandy Smith, Gary Ledbetter, Bill Needham, Mike Gilpatrick, Linda Carlen, Ethan Nivens, Rachel Nivens, Jim Nivens, Maisie Newberry, Maxine (Garrett) Nivens, Agnes Moore via Chris Coil, Jerry and Gina Hall, Cleston Daniels, Isabell Garrett, Illard Hunter, George L. Harris, W.C. Smith, Kenneth Dodson, and Gail Jones via Kim Garrett. Still other contributors not mentioned here are included in the commentaries and stories.

In closing I leave you with this old, **old saying** heard often during my childhood: "So long, **see you in the funny papers.**" Then, if you are an old timer like me, you'll reply, *"Not if you come out first."*

About the Author

Edwin Garrett, a retired teacher, still resides in his beloved Cedar Grove Community of which he so fondly writes. With the exception of six years spent in Akron, Ohio working in the rubber industry, he and his wife, Peggy, a true Southern lady and the love of his life, still make their home within one mile of the place where he was born. The Garretts are the parents of three children, four grandchildren, and four great grandchildren and both often state that those eight off-spring of their children are truly "grand" and "great."

He has always enjoyed "people," thus collecting many of the words and phrases recorded in this book from those acquaintances. His extended family is made up of many individuals and friends whose words, phrases, and unique language expressions helped shape the thinking of a young boy growing up in rural middle Tennessee during the waning years of The Great Depression and throughout WWII.

Garrett has always been an active member of his community, his church, and civic organizations in the area. His life has been enriched and enhanced with friendships of former students who occupied his classrooms during the fifty-plus years he served as classroom teacher, principal, Superintendent of Schools, and various positions in educational services and administration. Many friends and acquaintances who know Edwin well have often heard him say that he never had a job he didn't like, and it was this philosophy that he tried to instill in his students. He always told his graduating classes, "Choose a profession you love and if you don't love what you do, choose something else."

Around 1944 he began a journey into country music and songwriting with the purchase of a $5 guitar that led him to form many new friends and lifelong relationships that he and Peg still cherish deeply. He has been heard to say that this hobby never earned him much money but has been worth millions of dollars in the peace, contentment, and relaxation it has brought to him. He states: "Music and singing have truly been a highlight of my life."

In 2013 Edwin finally retired from work for the third time thus ending a long, illustrious career in education. He now enjoys the leisure time he has earned and loves "watching" Peg work in her flowerbeds. They both enjoy bird watching and spotting new and different species of wild birds. Does he have any regrets about choosing education as a profession? "None!" Would he do it again? "Absolutely!"

Printed in the USA
CPSIA information can be obtained
at www.ICGtesting.com
LVHW052059201223
767015LV00011B/103